Sir Francis C. Burnand

The ZZG or Zig Zag Guide

Round and About the Bold and Beautiful Kentish Coast

Sir Francis C. Burnand

The ZZG or Zig Zag Guide
Round and About the Bold and Beautiful Kentish Coast

ISBN/EAN: 9783337191511

Printed in Europe, USA, Canada, Australia, Japan

Cover: Foto ©Andreas Hilbeck / pixelio.de

More available books at **www.hansebooks.com**

The ZZG or Zig Zag Guide round and about the Bold and Beautiful Kentish Coast

Described by F C Burnand and illustrated by Phil May

London
Adam and Charles Black
1897

"Simple Arcadians both."

CONTENTS

PREFACE

CHAPTER I
PAGE
STARTING-POINT 9

CHAPTER II
RAMSGATE 11

CHAPTER III
ON BOARD THE GOOD SHIP "LAVEROCK" 23

CHAPTER IV
HINTS AND SUGGESTIONS 37

CHAPTER V
STILL AT RAMSGATE . . . 44

CHAPTER VI

To Pegwell 50

CHAPTER VII

About Ramsgate Harbour . . . 58

CHAPTER VIII

Quitting Ramsgate . . . 64

CHAPTER IX

Fordwich . . . 75

CHAPTER X

En Route for Margate . 81

CHAPTER XI

Sandwich 84

CHAPTER XII

Sandwich (*continued*)—"My Old Dutch" 92

CONTENTS

CHAPTER XIII

PAGE

ASH 102

CHAPTER XIV

DEAL 108

CHAPTER XV

COASTING AND INLAND IN SEARCH OF BARFRESTON 113

CHAPTER XVI

TO ST. MARGARET'S BAY . . . 124

CHAPTER XVII

BROADSTAIRS 130

CHAPTER XVIII

TO MARGATE FROM RAMSGATE BY THE ELEVEN O'CLOCK BOAT, AND FROM MARGATE TO BOULOGNE 133

CHAPTER XIX

MARGATE 140

viii   ZIGZAG GUIDE

CHAPTER XX

	PAGE
WESTGATE	. 154

CHAPTER XXI

BARFRESTON 167

CHAPTER XXII

THE THANET HARRIERS . . . 182

Comfortably tucked up

PREFACE

Probably unnecessary

WHATEVER may be the opinions of our most trustworthy medicine men, I, — *moi qui parle*, — speaking from the considerable experience of well-nigh a quarter of a century's residence, — though not as yet qualified with the authority of "the oldest inhabitant," — am absolutely certain that, for the majority of my fellow London citizens there are no better health-restorers, and no more perfect "life-preservers," than those pleasant "seaside resorts," not sufficiently resorted to, because only partially known, on the Kentish Coast, ranging from Birchington or Birchingtown (which, from its name ought to be a town of Schools in association with preparatory academies at Whippingham) to Hythe.

"We," my artistic confrère, and self, henceforth to be known in Dickensian phraseology as "T'Otherest" and "T'Other Guv'nor," do not purpose travelling so far west on the coast as Hythe, or, if we should do so, it will be only to give it a "look-in," and then to take a short run inland, returning to Dover for dinner, and so back again to Ramsgate or Margate, zigzagging about, here to-day, gone to-morrow, back again the day after, and going somewhere else the day after that.

As to Margate and Ramsgate, the idea as generally received by the "hupper sukkles" is that they are places of resort for "trippers" only, and therefore to be religiously avoided by those whom "Providence has blest with affluence," if not with perfect health.

Erreur, mes amis! a mistake so great indeed, that in order to prolong your lives, in order to make your useful existence still more beneficial, and to give extra chances of turning useless lives into useful ones, we, T'Otherest and T'Other, devote ourselves to the mission of converting you to *our* views (you will see the artist's and you will read mine) for your present and future

PREFACE

benefit, appearing in this simile and connection as two modified Augustinians, whose great founder St. Augustine himself was the first visitor to this health-giving, life-preserving locality.

* * *

Augustin was a name of good omen to Ramsgate and Margate, — as the season when most people can come here is *in August*. And it is, more or less, historically certain that the time of the good man's arrival on these shores was the last of the summer months, since he is invariably alluded to in the ancient records as "our august visitor." There was no hotel at the time of his landing in the low ground between Ramsgate and Pegwell, or if one did then exist, it was not run by a company; it was probably but poorly patronised; and, alas! the visitors' book has not been preserved.

* * *

Let me assure everyone, crying it aloud from the Martello towers along the coast, that no holiday time can be better passed than at either Ramsgate or Margate, during what is called their "season"; provided always, and be it here expressed and understood, that

the climate, of either one or the other, agrees with you.

First.—If the climate be against you. IF, at Margate, you are as hopelessly bilious, in the strong northern air fresh from the North Pole, as are some people at Brighton (so hopelessly bilious as to be utterly incapacitated and compelled to remain in bed during their visit, only to quit it in order to return to town); *Secondly*, IF you feel much the same in the milder Ramsgate with its southern aspect, the north wind at your back; then, on these hypotheses, the sheltered Broadstairs may render your life happy; or you

PREFACE

may be benefited by the more secluded Sandwich, inland, with access to fine golf links, and sea at some distance; but neither Birchington nor Westgate will suit those between whom and breezes from the North Pole there is no sympathy.

* * *

Well-informed persons familiar with the geographical situation of Calais and Boulogne are, generally speaking, under a strange misapprehension as to the relative positions of Margate and Ramsgate, which are not " Siamese Twins." They are not inseparable as were Castor and Pollux, Balbus and Caius, Box and Cox, William and Mary, Hero and Leander, and other historical characters usually bracketed. Nor are they by any manner of means alike, as were the Two Dromios: on the contrary, so distinctive are their characteristics, that it would be ordinarily impossible for the least keen observer when in Margate to think he was in Ramsgate, or *vice versa*.

* * *

They are " poles asunder," though distant only

from each other a matter of eight miles or so by coast, and by about four or five across country. Of course there are more ways than one of going from Ramsgate to Margate, "the beaten track" being one that is very easily beaten by other tracks which are not convenient for the ordinary Thanet Fly, coach, or *char-à-banc*. But these secrets of the Enchanting Island—do not forget that you have the privilege of being in an island —shall be revealed, later on, during the course of these travels.

*

ADVICE GRATIS.—If you love the sea and "sea-scapes," and if you intend taking up your *residence* on this coast, do so at Ramsgate. And at Ramsgate, Westerly.

Why at Ramsgate? Because Ramsgate faces south.

As I write now, from my room facing the sea on the western coast, my aspect—or rather the house's aspect—is due south. A row of houses guards the Crescent's (private) Gardens against the forces of the north wind; we are partially protected by Beneficent Builders (who, in some respects, were duffers) from the east wind, and we are fairly amenable to the advances of the softer west. Ramsgate throughout the year is warmer than Margate, as Margate faces due north; and, when you are at the end of Margate

PREFACE

Pier, you can confidently state, as something you are not afraid to let the whole world know, and in order to put an end to any possible scandal, that *there is nothing whatever between you and the North Pole*.

* * *

This being so, if you are on the East Kent Coast for the summer months only, and if those summer months are abnormally hot, then, by all means lodge at Margate, facing north; or at Westgate, or at Birchington, both facing north-west; but Margate is the coolest and freshest of the three.

* * *

In winter, however, all things considered, Ramsgate for choice; and after Ramsgate, Broadstairs.

* * *

Broadstairs lies between Margate and Ramsgate, and though thus "lying," it can be trusted as a *via media*, where *tutissimus ibis*; which Latin phrase was translated by a learned school-boy who knew something of natural history as the "Ibis (called) the Safest," because, in prehistoric times,

A NOTE AT BROADSTAIRS

8 ZIGZAG GUIDE

when the bird was an uncommonly fine one with fine feathers, you were *safe* to meet him somewhere, and *he*, with his Daddy-long-legs-like legs and out-spreading wings, was easily off before the simple bow-and-arrow sportsman could possibly take aim. To Broadstairs, sheltered and much frequented in summer, we shall turn our footsteps "in due course."

Ramsgate Bank Holiday 11 A M

CHAPTER I

MOTTO FOR TOURIST, *suggested by Mrs. Glasse's celebrated receipt for hare-dressing*—
"First catch your train."

Another and a Supplementary Motto—
"The earlier traveller catches the early train."

*　*　*

Too much luggage spoils the journey.

*　*　*

An inquiry in time saves any amount of strong language.

*　*　*

Rule as to picking up information beforehand and subsequently acting upon it—
"Hear to-day, gone to-morrow."

*　*　*

"There is many a slip between the platform and a compartment."

*　*　*

When in doubt ask at the ticket-office.

ADVICE.— Do not travel, if you can possibly avoid it, by a crowded excursion train. Remember the Shakespearian stage-direction, consisting of two words, almost invariably in conjunction, i.e.—

"Excursions and alarms!"

* * *

"If I were you," quoth our friend Major O'Shaughnessy of the Gallant Boardinghousers, addressing himself to T'Other Guv'nor, and T'Otherest Guv'nor, "wanting to 'do' the coast and to have a little bit up your sleeve inland, I should take up my headquarters at Ramsgate."

"And those headquarters?" asked T'Other Guv'nor, the Literary Gent.

"And those headquarters," continued the gallant Major, "would be your basis of operations."

Whereat T'Otherest chuckled grimly, and T'Other did something more than smile.

"For a' that and a' that," we, T'Other and T'Otherest, determined to yield to *force majeure*; which is T'Other's way of saying that we saw no better plan of campaign before us than the one proposed, and there and then we decided to act on the disinterested Major's advice.

CHAPTER II

RAMSGATE.—To be reached direct by the London, Chatham, and Dover Line, by Whitstable, Herne Bay, Westgate, Birchington, Margate, and Broadstairs; or by the South Eastern Railway with something of a *circumbendibus* by way of Canterbury, Grove Ferry, and Minster. To those who long for the earliest glimpse possible of the ocean, I should recommend the London, Chatham, and Dover journey, with view of the Medway opening to sea, of the River Swale, which helps to isolate Sheppey, a glimpse of Ancient Whitstable, where they make up any number of oyster-beds, and where there are very rarely any "to let" even in the worst season; a "look-in" at quiet Herne Bay; a passing glance at the mysterious Reculvers in the distance; a bow to Birchington Bungalows; a visit to Westgate (three minutes *d'arrêt*); three more or so at Margate; a pause at Broadstairs ("all tickets ready"), during which you will have time to remark the Seaside Sanatorium, the many artistically-finished red-brick houses (or the tops of them) "standing in their own (small) park-like grounds," and, in a general way, the ups and downs of Broadstairs out-of-door life, with a monumental sea-mark in the distance which, though not on semaphoring terms with the one near Birchington, is somehow or other, I believe, a connection both of the North Foreland and of the neighbouring North Foreland Lighthouse.

Inland you will have noticed short cross-country cuts which delight the bold equestrian (if there are no stiles in the way, whereof there are very few in Thanet), and considerably reduce the length of the pedestrian's journey from north to south, since by these paths he can go "as the crow flies."

All this the observant traveller, seated close to the near-side window, will have noticed what time the tickets are being collected by the Broadstairian official; and then at the sound of the whistle the train will move on with increasing speed, until, towards the end of a gruesome tunnel, it pulls up with a jerk. It does not do to come rushing and screaming into Royal Ramsgate, nor to enter into the town all panting, puffing, and blowing. So the engine assumes such quiet dignity as beseems a locomotive arriving close to the spot whence, once upon a time, the Majesty of England, hight George the Fourth, took his departure from his own dominions to seek those of the Gay Gaul, and whither he returned none the worse, let us hope, for his trip by sea. Is there not an obelisk on the pier recording this memorable feat? Thus runs the inscription—

"*To George the Fourth, King of Great Britain and Ireland,*"—" Ireland " always seems added as an afterthought,—"*the Inhabitants and Visitors of Ramsgate*"—the inhabitants could not manage it among themselves, so the unfortunate visitors "*of* Ramsgate" were taxed: [the visitors *to* Ramsgate would have been more correct; you pay a visit *to* not "of" Ramsgate; but this may be hypercritical] "*and the Directors and Trustees of the Harbour*"—The "Trustees" modestly put themselves last, but depend upon it it was *they* who got up the subscription and erected the obelisk; in fact they were at the bottom of this obelisk;—"*have erected this Obelisk as a grateful record*"—of what?—pause to guess—and resume—"*of His Majesty's Gracious Condescension in selecting this Port*" had they been all wine-merchants they couldn't have been more grateful—"*for his embarcation,*"—we heard an old lady read it out aloud as "embrocation," and certainly these directors and trustees did "rub it in"— "*on the 25th September, in Progress to*

His Kingdom of Hanover,"—(there were no adherents of "the King over the water" among the subscribers to this monument)—"*and his happy return on the 8. Novbr. 1821*": so Hanover did not long detain its Monarch, who, at the time of his starting from Ramsgate, had reigned but a year and a half, and probably required a little change of air. Perhaps it was to settle some of his late Queen Caroline's affairs in Brunswick, to which place the poor lady's remains had been conveyed for interment in the previous month, that he took this journey. However, be this as it may, "The first gentleman in Europe" made the trip (and many other trips of a different character) aforesaid, and of it this Obelisk is the memorial. No one can object to this Obelisk as being "pointless." Just look at the top!

So much you may observe on entering "Royal Ramsgate," while waiting for your luggage to be put on the trap (there are plenty of conveyances, and one of the local papers will give you the tariff, which is not exorbitant), and "stretching your legs" after the two hours' journey *per* London, Chatham, and Dover line from Victoria, Holborn Viaduct, or Ludgate Hill.

N.B.—*There is a capital train every evening from Holborn, Ludgate, and St. Paul's, starting from the last-named station at* 5.12, *and arriving at Ramsgate* 7.5. *This, like "the Waverley Pen,"*

RAMSGATE

is a " boon and a blessing to men." Consult timetables and see that you get this train,[1] unless you travel by the Granville Express, which is earlier.

We, T'Other and T'Otherest Guv'nor, will not prejudice our clients in favour of any one part of Ramsgate over another. There is room for all, and there are rooms for all,—" pick 'em where you like," as the vendor of nuts in a barrow says,—and the price of apartments, lodgings, and of houses to let, varies here, as everywhere else, according to situation.

For those who wish to be *directly* on the sands, there are a few small houses built *in* the East Cliff *on* " the Marina." Apartments over shops.

Others who like the benefit of the upper air, with a comparatively short walk down to the sands, will locate themselves somewhere up above on the East Cliff, or will stay at the Granville Hotel, which is admirably situated, and where all the luxuries of the season, including various kinds of baths, are to be obtained, and where the *cuisine* is fairly satisfactory, though the arrangement of its *menus* might be improved, were it assimilated to those of any good Continental hotel. The *menus* of most English hotels are stodgy and uninviting.

---

[1] *Running still; and will probably be joined, en route, by another train from Victoria.*

A slight acquaintance with Sir Henry Thompson's excellent book on *Food and Feeding* (which proves its author to be a past-master in dinner-giving) would be of the greatest service to any Maître d'Hôtel, and the practical carrying out of the celebrated surgeon's directions would result in such a combination of variety with economy, as to prove a great attraction to many who are discouraged from dining at hotels by the inartistic and ordinary *menus*. The days of "the Ordinary" are long since past, except for some ancient "bagmen" or "travellers" who patronise old-fashioned "commercial houses."

※ ※ ※

What to do at Ramsgate.— April and May are two delightful months here. At this season there are only drives, rides, walks, boating, and fishing. But in June, July, August, and September there are plenty of steamers with early trips and late trips; and there are extra trains and cheaper tickets. There are no public lawn-tennis grounds; and

SLEEPING BEAUTIES.
(EARLY MORNING TRIPPERS ENJOYING THEMSELVES

AN IMPROMPTU BALL ON THE SANDS AT RAMSGATE.

SKETCH ON THE LAST ROCK.

the place is deficient in Baths such as "Brill's" at Brighton. There is only one public Bathing Establishment, and that is on the West Cliff, just at the commencement of the Royal Crescent Promenade. It is not sufficiently "up to date," and is capable, as I suppose, of considerable improvement.

Why the town councillors, who have laid out a large sum of money on a fine new road on the West Cliff, and on sham rockwork and artificial waterfalls on the East Cliff, and have laid out a very pretty "park" hidden away at the back of the town (West Cliff), should not have provided lawn-tennis grounds, as at Eastbourne, as at Ilfracombe, as at Bournemouth, and as at many other places I could mention, is a puzzle. Perhaps they may be "going to do it"; perhaps not. As to a *Brill*-iant Swimming Bath they probably argue—"Is there not the Sea, like the poor, always with us? Are there not the Bathing Machines? Are there not the Yellow Sands? Sure-ly our own people, and our visitors, will be content with these? What *can* they wish for more?"

RAMSGATE

"Catch the 'Laverock'"

In the Season.—You *can* be out of the bustle and turmoil of holiday-makers—who are everywhere, choose what spot on the coast you will—ay, even the solitaries of Birchington Bungalows complain of it—you *can* be all to yourself, or selves, and say nothing to nobody, if *you will go west.* The wise come from the east, and go west. *Verb. sap.*

***

Tips for Excursions.—The more "tips" you get, the further you can go, and the more you will be able to do.

***

Advice during the summer season.—Be an early bird. Catch the "*Laverock*" (or any other steamer, *vide* advertisement; only keep your eyes open), which starts from the pier at 7.30 A.M. punctually.

Immediately, call "Steward"! This sounds dolorous, but it presupposes the voyageur to be a first-rate sailor who only wants to see the steward in order that that ready-handed official may receive instructions as to breakfast.

Sketch on the Laverock

Order it for eight o'clock punctually, and then as you walk the deck and enjoy the seascape, the landscape, and the refreshing breeze, you will own that now at least, and under these conditions, is "Life worth Living"!

Another Tip.—Never at any time during the season is there a crowd on this boat at its earliest voyage, starting 7.30. There may be perhaps twenty passengers; there may be forty; but what is this number on board a boat capable of carrying eight hundred or more? The summer season is not a long one. By mid September 'tis a thing of the past.

Besides you may depend upon it that the majority of these have brought their "refreshments" with them, or have breakfasted before coming off. We have done this trip over and over again, and never, including our own party of four or eight, have we seen more than another eight at breakfast. We backed our "eight" against theirs, and won easily. Frequently we have had Stewards and Saloon all to ourselves, in company with the genial Captain, thorough type of a bronzed seaman, to take the chairmanship (he is never thoroughly at home except in a "ship" of some sort) and be our "Autocrat of the Breakfast Table."

And what a breakfast! Excellent! And what appetites! Wonderful! Eggs, ham, steak, always the very best, and chipped potatoes (fancy this at 8 A.M! and feeling that you want it, and that you wouldn't be happy if you didn't get it), coffee, tea, toast, omelette, bacon, jam, marmalade, and any cold meats or chicken! All this for 2s. per head! and a gratuity to the steward *ad lib.*

How sweet our post-prandial pipe on deck, as, at a fair pace gliding by quaint old Deal, we waft a kiss to Black-Eyed Susan, and then, on Walmer Castle coming in sight, we talk of Nelson and the Iron Duke; finally our theme is the present pleasures and the probable future of St. Margaret's Bay, where, through glasses, we can see the two rival hotels, the bungalows, and a few boats, but not a living soul about, for the blinds are down, and as yet St. Peggy's Bayites are in the arms of Morpheus.

By 8.45 we are alongside Dover Pier. Ostend boats and Dover-and-Calais boats are waiting. There is some life hereabouts, but not much, for Dover doesn't rise with the lark, and except for a few employés rubbing (so to put it) the

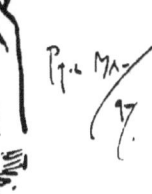

Apparitions at Dover

eyes of the New Lord Warden Hotel (which, being now an appurtenance of the Gordon Hotels Co., might, as Mr. Punch put it, have been rechristened " The Lord Gordon Hotel") there is scarcely a soul stirring anywhere on shore.

* * *

But on the pier 'tis different. Here some of our cargo disembark and the vacancies are filled by double the number, for now the gallant *Laverock* is going to be crowded. On our return voyage, a considerable number come on board at Deal Pier; and on Ramsgate Pier, which we make at 10.30, there is a big crowd waiting; and a bigger at Margate, from which point about midday the *Laverock* will finally quit the Isle of Thanet for her London-bound voyage, and she will discharge her passengers at Tilbury, or Gravesend, or Greenwich, somewhere about 4.30 or 5.

But we, the early birds of Ramsgate, who came on at 7.30, then breakfasted aboard, and came off at 10.30, will have had the very cream of the day. I don't know if early birds, or any other birds, take cream, — but this is a detail.

* * *

N.B.—Do not, if you are only a fairweatherly good sailor, miss this trip, which is one of the easiest, best, most health-giving, and most economical that can be done *from Ramsgate only*. Note emphatically, *from Ramsgate only!*

CHAPTER III

ON BOARD THE GOOD SHIP "LAVEROCK"

As you will be occupied with breakfast during the greater part of the trip from Ramsgate to Dover, when returning you must keep your eyes open.

Always carry a light field-glass. Less than a guinea will provide you with a very good one, sufficient for most purposes, if you select it carefully. Choose a light one of aluminium. Pocketable.

Note extension of harbour works at Dover; you won't see much, but you can imagine a lot. Dover Castle; coastguard station; convict prison, most healthily situated; the convicts were brought here to assist in the new Dover harbour works; but their labour is no longer

A passenger on the Laverock

A PASSENGER ON THE LAVEROCK.

required. Hence I believe no convicts are now in residence. These are matters of conversation for you with your occasional fellow-travellers, some of whom may be wiser (if this be possible) than yourself. Should you come across "The Well-Informed Man," who knows everything, *then* you may be perfectly certain that not one single item of his gratuitous information can be relied upon. Unless, of course, you like to repeat it afterwards to some one else who may be thirsting for knowledge, in which case you will have *re-lied* (with additions) upon the original.

* * *

St. Margaret's Bay, already noticed. When you passed it at 8.30 or thereabouts it was a picture of "Still Life," but now at 9.30 the saintly Margaretters are (nearly) "all alive O," and the cry of the bathers is after the manner of the warlike Hebrews, "To your tents, O Israel," though, as I have had occasion to remark, this war-cry would be more applicable to the majority of bathers at Margate.

* * *

Two-thirds of the residents and visitors now at St. Margaret's Bay are on the beach bathing or about to bathe. There are no bathing machines; tents only. *N.B.*—The grand total of residents and visitors at any one time cannot exceed forty or fifty all told. Therefore the St. Margaret's Bay company is limited and select. "*Elle grandira!*"

Keep your glasses up to your eyes as did the Great Duke at Waterloo, whose castle, that of Walmer, is the next "object of interest." Now 'tis Lord Salisbury who can, if it so please his Wardenship, reside there as Warden. The Gladstonians of the place salute his Lordship with "Ha! Warden!" But this is satirical, and though Lord Salisbury invariably smiles at the joke, yet, it is said, he never entirely forgives the witticism. By this time, however, he may be beginning to get accustomed to it.

"Next, please." Deal, Deal Castle, Deal Beach; Deal Pier. Quite the i-deal of "wooden walls" of Old England; *all Deal.*

Also suggestive of games of cards.

Stop at Deal Pier; take in cargo of passengers *en route* for Ramsgate, Margate, and London. A crowd! Well provisioned with baskets and bottles.

Passenger on the Laverock
"Storage of force"

Independent Laverockian *lunching* per se

Under-Steward paces deck, with tray beneath his arm, murmuring persuasively "Orders, please."

When Under-Steward's business falls off in consequence of the amount of provisions brought on board by the passengers themselves, then he is ready to do a bit in hatguards. 'Tis "an ill wind that blows nobody any good," and the worse the wind the better for the Under-Steward, who has any quantity of elastic strings attached to the lappel of his coat. With these, in a moderate north-easter or south-wester, he drives a prosperous trade. They are purchased eagerly and gratefully; and the most eccentric hats soon become strongly attached to them.

Talking of refreshments, what odd things persons of a certain class eat and drink on board ship by way of "saving life at sea"! Here is a respectable elderly man with a gray beard munching a yellow bilious-looking cake. By his side are deposited a small toy tin pail and a toy spade, suggestive of there being a grandson somewhere about; if so, this is Grandpapa eating the cake when Grandson isn't looking. Many have packets of buns, and bottles of lemonade, or bottles filled with mysterious brown liquor, —which may be cold tea " with a dash "; —and not a few have stone jars; some carry case-bottles, and some large flasks; but nearly all carry pies of some sort, mostly of pork, except those conscientious holiday-makers whose ancient eastern origin speaks through their noses, *et qui*, as to the pork, *n'osent pas*.

* *

Deal present, Deal past; what Deal future will be we have no time to guess; then ruined Sandman Castle with a history; after which note the Deal Golf Links, not the Sandwich ones which are superior to all other Golf Links, so authorities say, except those of St. Andrews. On our left hand as we turn towards Ramsgate we catch sight of Sandwich, in the distance, some three miles inland; while on our right, if the day, and our vision, be clear, we see the coast of France " t'other side of the water." Then Pegwell, celebrated for its shrimps; private houses in well-wooded grounds, well-wooded that is for

LIFE BOAT COX-
AT D

Phrenology at Ramsgate

the Kentish Coast; next, West Cliff Terrace, which has a fine lawn in front of it and a happy future before it, as its past is somewhat sad. Here we obtain a glimpse of the Convent of the Assumption, and of more private and "park-like grounds" down to the edge of the cliff. Finally comes in sight the tower of the house, and another tower belonging to the beautiful Gothic church, built by Pugin *père;* and in the background the Benedictine Monastery and College, occupying as healthy a situation as any parents could chose for their sons. Royal Crescent, with long line of houses, large winter garden, and promenade; then broken lines of houses; the Albion Club and the Thames Yacht Club finishing the upper portion overlooking the spacious new drive along the front, descending to the harbour, where, in the outer harbour, not the inner, we disembark at 10.30, bidding farewell to the civil skipper and his courteous crew. Here the gallant *Laverock* remains for one half-hour, in order to let some passengers debark, and to allow a crowd to embark,—the rule of the road being "One party off, t'other comes on,"—and then as the harbour bell sounds the stroke of eleven, steam is up, the Captain stands on the bridge, the steersman has his eye on the sea and his hand on the wheel—a genuine "wheel-man" this—and

Being photographed on the sands at Ramsgate
"Animated screen"

> Now they sail
> With the gale
> From the Pier of Ramsgate O !

* * *

But we, T'Other Guv'nor and T'Otherest aforesaid, remain to "do" Ramsgate, and for the sake of those who follow our wandering but trustworthy guidance, "to 'do' ourselves as well as we would have others 'do' *us*." Which is a new proverb quite up to date.

* * *

Fashions, manners, and customs have considerably changed even since Frith painted his popular "Ramsgate Sands" showing an idealised assemblage of most highly respectable persons in theatrically-arranged groups; and still more have they changed since the Duchess of Kent and little Princess Victoria dwelt at the back of the town, whence they drove up to London, the little Princess to become Queen, now in the sixtieth year, all told, of her happy and prosperous reign, and never again to set foot on this part of her Kentish dominions. It was in the early days of the Victorian era that Charles Dickens, while "a very young man," as he says of himself apologetically, in his later preface to the *Sketches by Boz*, published "The Tuggses at Ramsgate," wherein is shown how Mr. Joseph Tuggs, greengrocer, on the Surrey side of London Bridge, having suddenly come in for £20,000, at once put up the shutters and discussed with his family, consisting of his wife, daughter, and son Cymon, the problem as to where they should go in order to get rid, as it were, of the smell of the groceries, and begin a new and a fashionable life.

"Where should they go?"

"Gravesend," mildly suggested Mrs. Joseph Tuggs. The idea was unanimously scouted. Gravesend was *low*.

"Margate?" insinuated Mrs. Tuggs.

"Worse and worse—nobody there but tradespeople."

To Brighton there was the "insurmountable objection" that all the coaches had been upset in turn, and on an average there have been "two passengers killed and six wounded," and that in every case the newspapers had distinctly understood that "no blame whatever was attributable to the coachman."

"Ramsgate?" ejaculated Mr. Cymon thoughtfully, * * * "Ramsgate was just the place of all others."

Nowadays, indeed, the Tuggses still come down to Ramsgate, as why should they not, being highly respectable people, with perhaps a light-'arted 'Arry and a coquettish "Charlotta" in the

A Nosegay from Ramsgate

family party? But travel north, south, east, or west, 'Arry and 'Arriet and Tuggses of all grades and all counties are to be found, at Scarborough, Ilfracombe, Llandudno, Bournemouth, —everywhere, and all pretty much alike. Yet what's the odds as long as *they* are happy? and they are so happy for such a very short time! coming out of their stuffy shops and fluffy factories to get "a sniff of the briny," and to breathe the pure air and so get "a blow out" that will invigorate them, satisfy them, and make them better men and better women, happier girls, happier boys, and healthier babies, than ever they would have a chance of being in a vitiated atmosphere with noses perpetually down to the grindstone.

At certain seasons of the year, when a fresh lease of life is necessary, all these breathing-places are, and must be, and ought to be, crowded by those who pause in their toil to inhale the health-giving breezes, and then back again to drudgery with grateful remembrance, renewed hope and strength, and lighter hearts.

You can avoid Ramsgate on Bank Holiday, and stay in London; but Bank Holiday you will come across more or less everywhere out of town. Or, you can remain in Ramsgate high up on the West Cliff, and there, while enjoying the clear sea-view and the invigorating breeze, you can be as ignorant of the existence of Bank-Holiday surroundings as if you were spending a quiet day with a diver—or a *diva*, a "diving belle" for choice—at "the bottom of the deep deep sea."

"*O my Honey,*" sung to the "*M*" *Lasses on the Sands*

CHAPTER IV

HINTS AND SUGGESTIONS

I HAVE said "*starting at 7.30 by the boat.*" I daresay all the big boats are just as good as is the *Laverock*, but, without any intentional disrespect to the *Royal Sovereign*, this vessel, the *Laverock*, happens to be the one with which we, pilgrims of the sea and land, are best acquainted. Rather a "roller," which mayhap, my messmates, will not suit those who don't care about a roll with their breakfast. If the sea is calm then you go, *bercé* by the gentle undulation, "Laverock'd in the cradle of the deep."

* *

Of course it *is* difficult to "plough the seas" with a roller, but the gallant *Laverock* overrides all such obstacles.

* *

The *Oriel*, belonging to the same Company, is another good boat, running alternately with the *Laverock*. N.B.—The lavatory department in both is capable of vast improvement. Their model should be the Dover and Calais (L.C.&D.) new boats, as, during the time the Ramsgate and London boats are running, they must carry comparatively just as many passengers as do those of the Anglo-Continental Service.

* *

Says T'Otherest, pocketing his note-sketch-book with the decided air of a Wellington shutting up a telescope with a snap before uttering the memorable words, " Up, Guards, and at 'em ! " (which if he didn't, he ought to have uttered), " No doubt of it ! the East Cliff from the commencement of the Granville Hotel to the east end of the promenade ". —

"Which is still uncompleted, so characteristic of Ramsgatian management," interrupts T'Other.

" Very likely, but there it is, or isn't," resumes T'Otherest, "and anyhow this East Cliff, whichever way you look at it, from the shore level, or from the neglected East Pier "—

" Another Ramsgatian characteristic," puts in T'Other sarcastically.

" 'The East Cliff," continues

T"Otherest emphatically, "with its trees, shrubs, flowers, well-kept gardens, red-brick houses, and open green spaces, is picturesquely superior to the West Cliff, always excepting the Pugin House, the Gardens, and the Gothic Church."

"I agree," responds T"Other. "But had the West Cliff been throughout animated by the Puginesque spirit, then, possessing as it does a large private lawn and legal protection against all hawkers, wandering musicians, howling newspaper-boys, and importunate vagrants, the original freeholder (it is all freehold) should have built artistically-designed detached houses, say twelve of them, instead of the eighteen now stuccoed together, as if they had come out of a box of old-fashioned toys and depended on each other for support, and, had this been done years ago, the same West End of Ramsgate, with such trees and shrubs as are luxuriant in the Pugin and West Lodge Gardens, would have been 'hard to beat' by any other frontage along this coast."

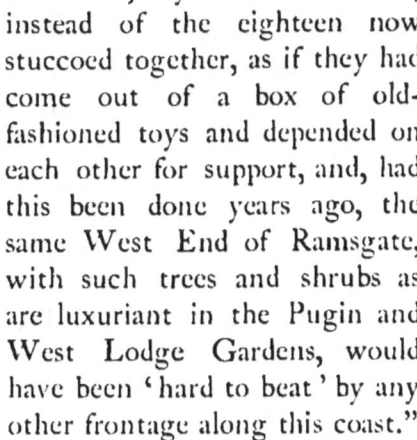

Evening Pee+Par

"*Out for a Blow*"

"True," quoth T'Otherest, "building terraces and crescents in the air is dry work. Stranger, it is 'two bells,' let us liquor."

                * * *

To the Casual Visitor, thinking of becoming a resident, the above conversation may be useful.

                * * *

The New Pier, many years old by now, for entrance to which, as being something superior, twopence is charged, is an instance of that kind of half-fulfilled promise whereof Ramsgate generally offers several evident examples. But while there is a pier there is hope, and it may yet occur to its proprietors, or to the local authorities, to say, after the manner of Mr. Wemmick, out of office-hours, in *Great Expectations*, "Hallo! Here's a pier! Let's do something with it!"

                * * *

At present, whoever, in the season, wants to lounge, with or without book or newspaper, in comparative quiet, let him pay his twopence and up the pier he goes. In winter it is solitude and well worth twopence to The Thinker.

                * * *

What would not a little enterprise do for this same pier?

   1. A good and sufficient Lavatory. All modern improvements and plenty of 'em, just as they now have at the entrance to the Old Pier and Harbour.

HINTS AND SUGGESTIONS

SKETCHED AT RAMSGATE
NOT A VERY SUITABLE COSTUME FOR AUGUST

2. A Newspaper Kiosque on the pier.

3. Let the Messrs. Anybody (but the Proprietors of the Granville ought to take it in hand, as they could work it inexpensively and effectively) start a first-class restaurant at the pier-head on the model of the one on Boulogne Pier (as it was, before it was spoiled), where a good *déjeûner à la fourchette* should be obtainable from eleven to three, band playing the while; refreshments in same style *à l'Américaine* all day; no waitresses, good waiters, and *dîner à la carte*, or *dîner du jour*, from 6 P.M. till 9.

Let it be managed as well as the Buffet at Calais Hôtel Terminus is managed, or as satisfactorily as you will find it done at the Restauration on the Calais Plage; and this, becoming known, will attract a large number of first-class visitors, who otherwise would not prolong their stay at the Granville, or who might not visit Ramsgate at all.

There is a comparatively quiet bathing-place just to the east of this pier where, there being no place for machines, there is plenty of opportunity for letting out temporary tents. At present it is given up to little paddlers.

* * *

Note.—Bathing at Ramsgate, at low tide, good but crowded. Best in the very early morning, tide and weather permitting. From Old Pier to Marina, old style; bathing-machines. From after New Pier, going east, informal. Take your own tent and be happy. Excellent bathing for paddlers and swimmers at Dumpton Gap: *but* take your own towels and folding umbrella tent, easily carried.

* * *

Why does not some enterprising speculator begin with a few tents on hire, a spirit-lamp boiler and pans (as in France), with some cans of fresh water, easily obtainable close at hand? Surely this bathing-tent speculation might be tried *tent*atively.

* * *

The range of the power exercised by the Warden of the Cinque Ports extends to Essex. Brightlingsea on the Colne, 11¼ miles from Colchester, is still a "Liberty of the Cinque Port of Sandwich."

THE INVALID.

HINTS AND SUGGESTIONS 43

Rather a substantial combination, "Port" and "Sandwich."

* * *

Broadstairs is a "Liberty of Dover." That is, it has a liberty of its own. "Who will be free themselves must strike the blow."

* * *

In the Churchyard of St. Peter's, Ramsgate, is to be seen the tombstone of Richard Joy the Kentish Samson, who was born in 1675 at St. Lawrence. A memoir of him appeared in *Sketch* for 26th August 1896, wherein it is said "*he partly supported himself by pressing his arms on a railing.*" That he was not able to "support himself" on land by fair means is evident from his having taken to the seafaring business of a smuggler, and, during a storm, his inability to "support himself" in the water was proved by his being drowned. Altogether, though at one time "going strong," an "insupportable sort of person."

CHAPTER V

STILL AT RAMSGATE

Thoughts on the pier at Ramsgate.—Is it possible for any man, or any two men together, to enjoy a holiday when both of them have alternately to take charge of a baby? Probably baby's father and baby's uncle. Father carries it while uncle wheels perambulator or go-cart; and so on, turn and turn about, until baby's bed-time, when mother will have to stop with it, and uncle and father may go out for a relief in larks. Or, father has to stay at home with mother and child; or father remains in and uncle and wife go out. However, 'tis a poor heart that never rejoices. Yet this and other lower-middle class family trips "of pleasure" cause me to wonder where on earth "the pleasure" comes in!

* * *

Just a little outing. Train from Ramsgate to catch 11 o'clock boat at Dover for Calais. Lunch at the *Gare Maritime*: no better anywhere, and you can *now* do it at your ease since you will have from 12.15 to 3. At about ten minutes to 3 there is a train which will drop you at Calais-Ville station; but if you are uncertain of this, order beforehand, by telephone (which either M. Wattlebled, *patron de la Restauration à la Gare Maritime,* or his manager, M. Carini, will place at your disposal), a *voiture* to await you. In this go to Calais-Ville station. Start at 3.26 for Étaples, *par* Boulogne, where you will have to wait about an hour; time enough to take a *voiture et faire la tour de la ville* and return. You will arrive at Étaples at a little before six, whence take fly or omnibus for the Grand Hôtel at Paris Plage. Here stay the night. Next morning visit Montreuil, next station after Étaples, and drive up to the Grande Chartreuse well worth seeing; visit the old churches, and return to Paris Plage for the night, getting the benefit of the sea air and the delightful quiet (there is nothing to do), and then return by the 11.26 train from Étaples, back by Boulogne to Calais, then to Dover, and arrive at Ramsgate in time for 8.15 dinner.

* * *

Another outing.—Do a third of the above. Calais and back; with three hours at Calais.

* * *

Another by sea (this is a very cheap and pleasant

Sketched at Dover Castle
"Ow, 'Arry, what a 'at!"

STILL AT RAMSGATE

trip).—To Boulogne by *La Marguerite*. Stay the night and back next day *via* Calais boat to Dover.

* * *

Another by sea.—To Dunkerque. Stay the night at Rosendäel, which is a few minutes, per train, from Dunkerque, and return next day *via* Calais and Dover to Ramsgate. Always back (at latest) for dinner at Ramsgate 8.15.

* * *

The boats, if not too crowded, are very good; the passage ordinarily fair; feeding satisfactory; and the expense is about one-third of what it would be per rail and sea.

* * *

For my part I include such trips as among the possible amusements of any seaside place; and no seaside place is worthy of the name unless it can offer the attraction to its visitors of *getting away from it* by good steamboats, and so returning. A seaside place without a pier, without shipping, without steamers visiting continental and home ports, is not worthy of the name. Maritime advantages should be things *per se* at a seaside resort.

* * *

The *Ruby*, belonging to the Steamboat Company Limited, used to do the Southampton to Havre passage. It is a capital sea-going boat. From Ramsgate and Margate the *Ruby* makes a variety of sea-trips. It goes to Hastings, St. Leonards, and Eastbourne. Keep your eyes open for the announcements and make inquiries of everybody at all likely to be "in the know." Otherwise, as it seems, the policy of Ramsgate authorities is to keep these things hidden from the dwellers on the East and West Cliffs, only partially revealing them to favoured ones on the pier. The casual visitor may remain in unblissful ignorance of the above facts, and quit Ramsgate protesting indignantly.

* * *

These boats go to Deal and Dover and Dungeness. To Boulogne and back; to Dunkerque; round about the lightships and the heavyships, without any hardships.

* * *

The *New Palace Steamer Company Limited's La Marguerite* does Boulogne and back. The *Royal Sovereign* does the same occasionally; and their regular voyage is from Old Swan Pier, London Bridge, South Woolwich, and Tilbury, to Margate, Ramsgate, Deal, and Dover. What can any one wish for more?

* * *

Also start by the 7.30 A.M. "Laverock" for Dover and you can board a steamer there for Ostend. See Ostend, lose or win your money, and return by next boat.

All these advantages of foreign travel with only a *sac à la main*, and your *pied à terre* in your English home at Ramsgate!

※ ※

There are sailing boats for those who merely want to go out for a blow. Sometimes it is rather a knock-down blow.

※ ※

Capital fishing off Ramsgate, some way "off"; and for a couple of shillings, with any luck, you can supply your table for breakfast, lunch, and dinner with the best of fish.

CHAPTER VI

TO PEGWELL

A short walk.—To Pegwell and back. Away out from Ramsgate by the West Cliff. Pass Mr. Warre's place and later Westcliff Terrace, which ought to be taken in hand, pulled down and built up again with just half the present number of houses. Then pass Mr. Martin Tompson's grounds and house (looking uncommonly well from the sea), and on by another private house and grounds on the left, which is the last before we enter Pegwell, a village of one short street and several houses of entertainment for men, beasts, and shrimpers.

Pegwell is the grave of large ideas: Here were to have been pleasure-grounds, swimming baths, *al fresco* dining bosquets, summer-houses for tea-parties, for lunching-parties. Once upon a time a long pier was commenced intended to run far out over the muddy sands, so that visitors, coming in boats, could debark after a pleasant

sail and disport themselves in the Gardens of
Pegwell. But the money ran out before the
pier did, and so the idea was nipped in the bud.
Shrimps were to be the *specialité* of the Pegwell
Gardens, likewise dishes were to be served up
with samphire pickled—which to gather fresh
and unpickled was the "fearful trade" of its
gatherer as described by one William Shakespeare. Then potted shrimps were to be there
to tempt you, fresh from the celebrated purveyors
and picklers of shrimps, yclept Mr. Banger (and
family), who could be at almost any time caught
red-handed (so to speak) at this peculiar line of
business. There was to have been such bread
and butter as never had been dreamt of! there
were to have been such "high teas!!" And
for exercise, besides bathing, rinking, and tennis!
there was to have been a hotel for those who
came to stay, and good stabling and, in fact, it
was intended that Pegwell should be towards
Ramsgate what Deauville was to Trouville, and
was to be of far greater value to Ramsgate
than is Broadstairs to either Ramsgate or Margate . . . in fact there was a Great Future for
Pegwell! * * * when, suddenly, it all collapsed
—the half-finished tea-houses became mouldy,
the swimming-bath ran dry and green, moss
grew on the steps the roof of such buildings
as had been erected tumbled in, the walls

crumbled, and idle boys up above derived much amusement from throwing down stones and gradually breaking the glass. The commencement of the pier was broken up by a rough and angry sea which would not be trifled with; the hotel windows cracked, so did the stable (it ought to have been advertised to the racing world as a "stable full of cracks"); so did every one who had anything to do with it, all went cracky, and finally, "bang went saxpence!"—the splendid scheme had vanished into thin air, like the castles in Prospero's speech. "We know what we are, but we know not what we will be," quoth the Immortal Bard, who had visited Kent, and there may yet be a brilliant future in store for Pegwell; only the sooner Mrs. Future brings it out of her store-cupboard, the better, probably, for Pegwell.

* * *

When at Pegwell purchase at Banger's a bottle of Samphire pickle. It is an excellent relish and, as far as I am aware, but little known out of Thanet. The mention of the Immortal Bard in my foregoing note reminded me of it. A "pretty pickle" occasionally must the samphire-gatherer be in himself, if he still pursues his "dreadful trade," as apparently he was accustomed to do in the sixteenth century.

Pass through Pegwell and take the walk along the cliff (not *over* the cliff) to Cliff's End, where is a fine estate and big house. Ask at the Lodge, and the lodge-keeper will show you all over the place if nobody is there. It has a somewhat curious history, quite modern, which you can hear on the premises. Should there be no lodge-keeper, also no dogs about, likewise no gardeners, and no one in the mansion, then you can show yourself over, free of charge. But – *mem.*— always be provided with a silver ticket, which, in the shape of half-a-crown, is a *passe partout*.

WHEN in doubt consult a sign-post. Lots of them about. Likewise milestones occasionally. If you are inclined for a walk, make for Manston, then double back to Ramsgate, which you will enter in triumph, passing by the Church of St. Lawrence, "which," as Mr. Toots observes, "is of no consequence,"—at least on this occasion, though it is rare to find any old country church in which there is not something to interest the visitor.

When at Cliff's End, in the meadow-land of Ebbsfleet, just without the gates of the property to which your attention has been directed, stands a handsome Runic stone cross, erected by Lord Granville and friends to mark the spot where St. Augustine landed. "But," writes Mr. Boys in the Sandwich MS., quoted by J. R. Planché in his book on *A Corner of Kent,* "it was at Ruplicester, or Richborrow, near the old city of Stonehore, that the King, sitting under the cliff, or rock, whereupon the Castle (of Richboro') is built, commanded Augustine and his followers to be brought before him."

* * *

Richboro' was Rutupis to the Romans and Rusberg or King's Castle to the Saxons. Now it is a place for picnickers. The only "remains" are the old walls, except after an incursion of picnickers aforesaid, and then some bones are found, and perhaps a coin or two. These last are very rare.

* * *

Apropos of Richboro'. Thorne, a monk of Canterbury, writes the name as "Ratesborough." An important place then, ecclesiastically, as being the "borough" where "Rates" were levied.

* * *

The river here was called "the Wantsum," and the low marshy land about was named the "Wantsum Moor." But 'twas the fate of the Wantsum to be swallowed up by the bigger River Stour. "Nobody Wantsum" and so the stream disappeared.

Will the tourist have the luck that befell T'Other Guv'nor who, some few years ago on the way to Pegwell, encountered the comely shrimping-girl, thenceforth to be remembered as " Peg of Pegwell Bay " ? Her auburn hair was " hanging down her back," her petticoats were short, her feet and ankles bare, as bare as those of any Boulonaise fish-woman ; she had strong but shapely, sunburnt hands, a neat waist, a regular profile, and such a light in her laughing eye as would be an attraction to the honest lover, and a warning to the piratically inclined.

* *

She is happily married. There is a small family of tiny children, " quite shrimps," says Peg laughingly, but she is no longer the shrimper, having removed from Pegwell and set up, for herself and husband, in a business not unconnected with that from which originally she derived her net profits.

TO PRETTY PEG OF PEGWELL BAY [1]

    Your legs are sturdy, shapely, tanned,
    Your face is brown, and brown your hand,
    You stride o'er sand and rock and boulder,
    Ever your net across your shoulder.
You do it in a business way !
My Pretty Peg of Pegwell Bay !

[1] The music to this song has been composed by Sir Alexander

You show no *chaîne* nor *boucles d'or*,
As wear your sisters on the shore
Of bright Boulogne, or *plage* of Calais.
You're not inclined to flirt or dally,
You sing and toil, but make it pay,
You Pretty Peg of Pegwell Bay!

You're thrifty, though you "make a splash,"
And all your earnings are "net cash."
Lucky the shrimper who can catch you,
'Tis rare to find a girl to match you!
Ah! Lassie! Ye'll be caught some day,
My Pretty Peg of Pegwell Bay!

You, bright, light-hearted, shrimping maid,
Will soon become a matron staid,
With little shrimps of children hopping
On bootless errands, dry or sopping.
Your mate will say, "I bless the day
I wedded Peg of Pegwell Bay!"

* * *

Prawns hereabouts are rare, and but poor things in comparison with the shrimps of Pegwell Bay, whose flavour, go where you will and "pick 'em where you like," may be equalled, but cannot well be excelled.

* * *

The *Stour*, which makes Thanet what it is, *i.e.* an island, derives its name from the old

Mackenzie, Mus. Doc., and is published by J. Williams of Berners Street.

Norman French jest (which is best rendered in modern form) about *La rivière qui fait ses tours*. Hence *Stour*. The old British word, *es dur* (meaning simply "water"), implies that all the water here was *dur* or hard.

CHAPTER VII

ABOUT RAMSGATE HARBOUR

FEW harbours are more picturesque than the inner one here, with its assemblage of fishing-smacks and ships of many nationalities, having put in for shelter, for business, for repair, or as their native haven of rest. Here you may see a spectral-looking vessel, all white, of strange build. Can it be the Flying Dutchman's demon craft, disabled during a recent gale, with masts damaged, bowsprit smashed, and in a general way the spell of its weird existence broken? No: it is an ice vessel. From a Nansenian expedition? Wrong again: it is merely laden with ice, which is landed *en bloc*, and can then be bought, at retail price, cheap; as can also be purchased the coals from the big barges, by those who take the trouble to hire a cart and fetch their own parcels. The coal vessel and the ice vessel very near each other; quite "a study in black and white."

Round about the harbour are to be seen enormous buoys, the very biggest buoys in existence, as if they had been designed and made to serve as "properties" for some nautical scene in a Drury Lane pantomime. Very idle buoys are they, doing no work, lying down, standing, propped up, all lazy and inert.

※ ※ ※

Stacks of timber for shipbuilding, storage-houses, mysterious machine houses, practicable bridges, dividing in the centre, for the egress and ingress of craft; vessels with confused rigging, most puzzling to a landsman; spiders of boys and sailors climbing about nautical webs— boys and sailors must be web-footed to achieve this so easily; shapely masts like the trees of a pine forest in winter; flags of various nations; quaint devices pictured on the bows; boat-hammering, boat-building, boat-repairing, on lines inclining towards the basin, into which they will presently be re-launched. Buoys unattached, floating wearily in all sorts of positions; small two-legged boys or "sea-urchins"; and small boats taking perilous voyages about the outer harbour; yachts in both harbours, trim, taut, and well found, along the East Pier, attracting much attention from the loungers; while on the West Pier there is one solitary amusement offered by the Harbour Authorities in the shape

Wind-Lasses

of a Camera Obscura, which can be seen—if the exhibitor is only to be found, but to find *him* seems to be a perpetual puzzle—for the small charge of threepence, and half-price for children. If it be true that the money taken at the door of this exhibition goes towards the support of the Lord Warden of the Cinque Ports, it is to be hoped he does not depend for the necessaries of life entirely on the income derived from this show. The nett result may give him a luxury or two, such as nuts for dessert, or an occasional dish of almonds and raisins, but the Warden will be wise if he looks for his regular income from other and less precarious sources.

* *

Wind-lasses with their tresses blown about in the breeze, wind-lads in the shape of breezy tars; huge rusty chains for binding sea-monsters; heavy dredgers worked by mudshipmites, bound for the Isle of Muck,—'tis the only place I can think of where they should ultimately disgorge; strange square boats from Bremen; Norwegian vessels with cleanly-looking houses built up on deck, as if they were colonising villages in England and bringing over a few cottages at a time; sea-dogs ashore explaining their own barques to other sea-dogs; a good deal of yarn-making everywhere when other trades are dull; a busy place, in a quiet way, waking up to a ringing of bells and a striking of clocks at stated times; and then a rush of people (there's a crowd to be got together here in a second, and dispersed as soon) to see a boat arrive, or to witness the departure of fishing-boats, — a beautiful sight when, after a storm, a whole fleet takes its departure for Northern Seas. Then falls a holy calm over everything and everybody about meal times; when even in the highest holiday season there is tranquillity, for at least an hour, on the harbour and on the sands—

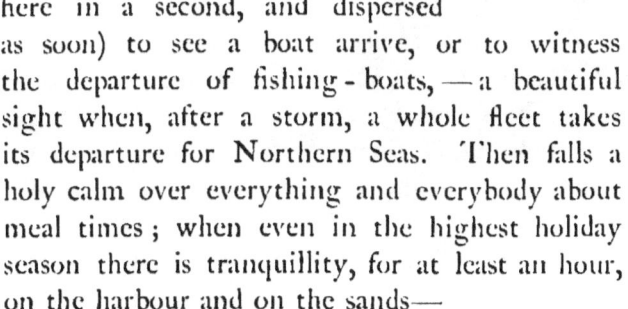

Buoys

> When the niggers have departed,
> And the beery are at rest.

* * *

The buoys again! Never was such a home for buoys! Black and white buoys, red buoys, variegated buoys, top-heavy buoys, rolled-over buoy lying along as if with pain in its side,—you can almost hear it groaning,—mitre-shaped buoys, as if calling to mind the old custom of "the Boy Bishop"; cannon-shaped buoys placed ready to go off; fishing-float-shaped buoys; bad buoys in cages imprisoned, and other irrepressible buoys in heavy chains like "the nobles" in "links of iron."

* * *

Cranes, chains, huge stones with grand iron stanchions, and preposterous iron rings wherewith sea-monsters might wed one another; rusty chains, pieces of iron, stacks of huge cables; and, quietly apart, in full view of everything going on, going off, going up, or going down, is the Harbour Guard's Watch House with, hanging on the walls, full printed directions for saving life at sea. Finally, horses and carts on the quay looking very much out of their element, unless you put them down as sea-horses and dog-fish carts.

* * *

And the perfumes! Sniffs of coal, whiffs of tar, faint odours of fishy packing-cases, appetising smells from cooking cabooses.

* * *

With the pleasure-boats *Moss Rose* and *Prince Frederick William* sailing out and sailing in, with the steamboats departing and arriving, with the little boats for amateur fishers and the big smacks, manned by professional crews, with the haulings and the heavings, with the landmariners, with the crowds on the sands t'other side of the harbour, with the coast view and the sea view, the most friendless man on earth will soon get into conversation with somebody about something, and the solitary stroller will effect a combination which may end in a pleasant evening, and even the half-confirmed bachelor may defer the ceremony of his full confirmation and surrender himself captive to some syren of the sands or some peerless peeress on the Pier.

Youth & Age a common sight at Ramsgate.

CHAPTER VIII

QUITTING RAMSGATE

On Pier.—Note persevering and enterprising babies who will insist on walking, or toddling, into all sorts of difficult places, and who are perpetually being either coaxed or threatened, petted or smacked.

* * *

Distracted mother to one baby who with suicidal intentions is craning over parapet, " You mustn't go over there "—child (sex uncertain to casual spectator) is quite angry at not being allowed to drown itself. " Now there's a dearie (*coaxing*), come and see Aunty Emma." Child doggedly refuses to yield even to the attraction of " Aunty Emma." It will move nowhere except seawards. At last it is dragged away by its mother, who has to attend to a few other wandering infants. " Now there's a dear, clever —why he's got 'old of the 'andle!! " (of a bucket half full of water which the precocious infant is

The Maccabees at Ramsgate

trying to upset over itself). "Come away from it (*angrily*), will yer?" But it won't. "I'll whip you in a second!" (*Child struggles with bucket. Mother and elder sister struggle with child. Desperate scene. Then mother very severely*)- "Will you play?" (*Shrieking at infant*)—"Will you be good?" (*Howls. Recalcitrant infant dragged away.*)

* * *

Yes indeed; as the Grossmithian burlesque of a Harrisonian recitation hath it, "*And the mother and the child are there!*" very much there, and here, and everywhere, during holiday-time at Margate and Ramsgate.

* * *

Exciting dialogue on pier when steamer is approaching: glasses out. "'Ere it comes!" "No, it don't!" "Yes, it do!!" "There you are!" "Lend me your glasses!" "Oh! I see." "Give 'em me." "*I* don't see it." "You're not looking right." "Oh! *Now* I do." "I shall watch it." "*I* shan't." And so on *ad infinitum*.

* * *

A good supply of steamers. The larger ones being comfortable, and might be in certain respects made still more so.

But these steamers have only a kind of ephemeral existence. For more than a day, it is true. They burst into life from about the first week of July—they may start before this, but not for *daily* trips—and continue running until the second week in September. I think the

daily trips to Dover and back do not commence before August: up till then the boats go only twice or three times in the week, there and back. If these boats were worked by a "Limited Company," imbued with modern ideas, a good deal might be done with them. At least so it appears to both T"Other and T"Otherest

Guv'nors, who, however, do not profess to be in "the know,"—but who are, in a General Steam Navigation sort of way, "all there or thereabouts."

* * *

What breakfasts at 8 A.M. on board the *Laverock!* Coffee (excellent), tea, fish, curry, eggs, steak and chips, jam, marmalade, toast, etc. etc. Sometimes a dish omitted, sometimes the "complements of the season."

* * *

What appetites! Captain Wells in the Chair. No better Captain; likewise carver, sees everybody well served and runs risk of being chopless, eggless, or steakless. When he *does* begin, give him time, not too much chatter. *Motto,* " Leave Wells alone."

* * *

The steamers have a short life and a merry one. They are here to-day and gone to-morrow; a two months' season at the utmost, "which," to quote the Pote with music by Sullivan—

> "Which seems a pity, a pity,
> Which seems to us a pity!"

* * *

Ashore at Ramsgate.—"Sharry bangs" with four horses, and smaller ones with a pair, in holiday-time, for tours round Island of Thanet.

QUITTING RAMSGATE

But why is Ramsgate avoided by the illigant four-horse coach that starts from Margate (apparently shies at Ramsgate) and goes here there and everywhere, *except* "Royal Ramsgate"?

* * *

Fathers, mothers, uncles, aunts, and children, in full force on every steamer, on the sands, on the pavement—everywhere—in the brief, very brief holiday-time.

This year all middle-aged tradesmen coming to these seaside resorts seem to have got themselves up after the now well-known portraits of President Kruger.

* * *

Advice to those holiday-enjoyers about to tour by land or by sea.—When in doubt take only a sunshade, or an umbrella. If sunshade alone, it *may* rain: if umbrella, depend upon it the weather will hold up and save you from holding up the umbrella. "Overcoats and umbrellas being intended *to ward off the rain*," the sage says, "take 'em—and the rain will be warded off." But there you are with lumber to carry about,—which is a nuisance.

* * *

Ramsgate ought to have a real good Swimming Bath worthy of the name. That at the Paragon on the West Cliff is not, at the present time

(1896), inviting to the first-class plunger. And thus it has remained for ever so long.

A first-rate "Brill's Baths," as at Brighton, required here. Swimming to be taught by a professor. It would be highly popular, and would be largely supported by the numerous schools and colleges.

* * *

Going to Margate from Dover, Deal, or

Ramsgate.—*Advice* as to steamer. Get on board early, and secure a portable seat at once. You can then place yourself wherever you like.

* *

Buns, bottles, and baskets are the provisions as a rule. For yourself, keep your eye on the steward, and the steward will pull you through.

* *

Parents, on board, must have a delightful time with "worriting" children. *Mother (shaking peevish child)*—"You won't let no one 'ave not no peace, will yer?"

* *

At starting of steamer, hark to the five minutes bell. Solemn sound as if summoning the passengers to prayers. "Steam Service" from Ramsgate to Margate at 11 A.M.

* *

With the exception of one bit where there is generally a space of sea-water about ten yards in length and from three to four feet deep, the bold equestrian can ride right away from Ramsgate to Margate, per Broadstairs, without once going inland. Delightful in spring and in winter. Too hot this ride for summer.

* *

To sum up :—Having nature's gifts the Local Authorities of Ramsgate are therewith content. How to develop these gifts so as to render

Ramsgate a place of resort, residence, and recreation for the Lower Five of the Upper Ten, seems at present beyond the resources of "Royal Ramsgate's" civilisation. The Wise Councillors, all, or nearly all, in trade, seem to say to themselves, "Have we not a New Pier (price twopence entry), an Old Pier (gratis), a drive, two bands (more or less tuneful), the sea, a park at the back (which when found can be made a note of), and what more could any one want? Isn't our climate so perfect that we do not care about taking our sewage farther and farther away out to sea, and thus doing all in our power to ameliorate the occasional whiffs with which in a southerly wind our atmosphere is occasionally flavoured?"

* *

Town Councilmen putting their heads together

But if the Town Councilmen would put their heads together (some persons would like to knock them together, but that would effect no good purpose) and decide on purchasing- -

Lawn-Tennis Grounds,

Then decide on erecting one good, central Bath House, with swimming bath *à la* Brill of Brighton, or as at Ilfracombe,

Starting a Golf Course somewhere—a little difficult to find, unless it be between Ramsgate

QUITTING RAMSGATE 73

and Broadstairs,—but it is only half an hour to Sandwich, where are the best golf links out of Scotland;

Then decide on improving the harbours, outer and inner, and then lighten the dues on yachts (but these are, I believe, matters for the Board of Trade), then, the above recommendation having been adopted, the Town Council might begin to congratulate itself.

Lunch at Calais

If there were some real good stabling, and some real good horses for hire, specially in the winter;

If the Junior Pier had on it a first-class restaurant served from the Granville;

If there were some first-class Concerts;

And if the means of communication—in spring and summer at all events—between Ramsgate and the coast of France (per Dover) were so arranged as to offer inducements to those who love a day's outing to go, without long delays, from Ramsgate at 10 A.M. to catch the 11 A.M. steamer; lunch at Calais and return by 3.45 boat, and be back at Ramsgate again by 6.30, in time for late dinner,—then, it strikes me, there would be, at Ramsgate, little to complain of, much to attract, and plenty to do.

* * *

The local papers ought to publish all the Railway time-tables, and besides, should have *one of their own* showing at a glance the means of communication, the times of the boats' departure, and in fact every sort of information for travellers and residents, who will forward the papers to " friends at a distance."

* * *

As it is, there are in the local papers the Time-tables, rendered somewhat puzzling by abbreviations and omissions, but with very little, if any, continental (*i.e.* Dover and Calais, Boulogne and Folkestone, Dover and Ostend) information.

'*You won't let no one 'ave not no peace, will yer?*'

The Ducking-Stool at Fordwich

CHAPTER IX

FORDWICH

From Ramsgate to Canterbury by South-Eastern Railway; from Canterbury to Fordwich by carriage, from Fordwich to Grove Ferry, and thence return to Ramsgate.

Canterbury. The Cathedral of course. If you can manage to visit it out of the tourist season, so much the better, and in this case see if you cannot get an introduction to a Canon, who, if he has not " gone off," as canons are apt to do—for his holiday—and is in residence, will furnish you with a special "*passe partout*," and you will see all that there *is* to be seen without reserve. Only, mind you, to this you must give a day, and make two visits, morning and afternoon, with lunch between whiles at the County Hotel, where everything appears to be done in good style. The picturesque entrance hall of this hotel is so arranged as to make a commodious and comfortable smoking‐room, where the inferior sex can enjoy their tobacco without being deprived of the charm of female society, as the ladies are not necessarily under sentence of banishment to that genteel purgatory known as "the Ladies' Drawing-Room." Thank goodness, in this respect our hotels are becoming every year more civilised.

* *

There are plenty of local guide-books to the Cathedral, and every day, Sundays excepted, officials are at hand, charged with the duty of conducting parties over the Cathedral. If possible, go as "a party" by yourself. There are several curiosities in the Cathedral that even the most learned are at a loss to explain. Among these are the grotesque carvings on the pillars in the crypt. One of these represents a goat playing a flageolet, and being painfully interfered with by a huge fish, while a kind of devil with pig's feet is performing on a fiddle. The introduction of the "fish" above mentioned would seem as if there were some monkishly humorous reference to the musician practising his scales.

At Canterbury hire a trap and drive to Fordwich, where you will see the old Town Hall. It is now a mere barn, of which the keys are kept at the neighbouring public-house. Notice the prison underneath the session-room, and then walk out and see "The Ducking-Stool" suspended over the river.

The prospect of such a rough-and-ready punishment always available at the shortest

78 ZIGZAG GUIDE

possible notice must have checked many a nagging tongue.

"O Goody, please to moderate the rancour of your tongue,"

at least when at Fordwich, or else—"The Ducking-Stool."

Pretty bit of river here. Hire a boat and row down to Grove Ferry, or up to Canterbury.

The sport here is limited. There are fish: also rats.

In the old Church at Fordwich are still to be seen the ancient pews, and among them the pew of the Mayor of Fordwich, with rests for the mace. The Mayor was, once upon a time, an important personage, in respect of his office. Some quaint old carvings on pew.

In a corner see a very old tomb with pillars beautifully carved. It is supposed to be that of the Founder of this Church. Many years ago it was removed to Canterbury Cathedral, but, as the latter possesses a wealth of curiosities, this tomb was kindly restored by the ecclesiastical authorities to its place in Fordwich Church. This is a remarkable instance of "the restoration of an antique" (to its lawful owners), and it is still in an excellent state of preservation.

"*When in doubt take only a sunshade, or an umbrella*"

There is a font as old as the oldest part of this Church.

As the "scraping" process has been

commenced, probably some ancient decorations may be found. The path up to the Church is rather muddy, as in bad weather are also the roads, so the pedestrian will be glad to assist in the "scraping process" before entering the porch, where he will find the scraper, always at hand, or rather at foot.

* * *

Here, too, may be seen the Royal Arms with the Commandments, Creed, and Lord's Prayer all on one board, which, removed from their original position over the Communion Table, are now fixed high up above the Chancel Arch. The subtle symbolism of this position seems to signify that the Commandments, though honoured aloft, are, in a general way, above the heads of the people: at least they certainly are over the heads of the good people of Fordwich.

* * *

Some deep-coloured stained glass in window, but the meaning intended is as deep as the colour.

"*All middle-aged tradesmen coming to these seaside resorts seem to have got themselves up after the portraits of President Kruger.*"

CHAPTER X

EN ROUTE FOR MARGATE

A CONFIDING friend has lent me (*Advice to the Book-possessors*, "Never lend, Always borrow") a delightful old book called "Pictures of Margate," published in 1820 by Messrs. Baldwin, Cradock, and Joy of Paternoster Row.

"Where is that barty now?"

Yet 'twas a partnership that ended with Joy! The writer says of Margate in his preface—

"A TOWN so much resorted to not only for the benefit of sea-air and bathing, but even for the sake of pleasure, is well worthy the attention of the topographer, and the pencil of the artist." Is not "even for the sake of pleasure" delicious?

* * *

In 1896-97 it is T'Other Guv'nor and T'Otherest who are respectively the Topographic and the Tip-Top-o-graphic Artist.

Whence came the name of " Thanet "? It is supposed that a Greek Colony, probably a Greek travelling company with Greek plays, came, and, liking it, settled here. Then, on account of its marvellous salubrity, the managers of the Colony, wishing to attract others and to make good business of the "spec," entitled it "Athanatos," or "The Deathless Island."

        * * *

"Well," observes T'Otherest Guv'-nor sagely, "from my own experience of what I've seen in driving, and what I have personally come across in riding, I should say that *a Thanet 'oss* is about as deathless an animal as they make 'em. Just ask a Fly-proprietor or a Livery stable-keeper."

        * * *

Or, the name came from the Saxon *Thacnet*, signifying "moist" or "watery." But the climate as a rule is neither "moist" nor "watery." The average of rain is less in Thanet than it is —almost anywhere.

        * * *

This interesting old book enumerates all the advantages of being a "Cinque Port." One is "Exemption from rates and taxes."

There were very many other notable advantages accruing to Cinq Ports, in return for which "The Cinque Ports were required to fit out fifty-seven ships each manned with twenty-one men and a boy." The "boy" settled it. Ramsgate could supply the men and the ships, but couldn't part with the "boy." So this privilege is defunct: but rates and taxes still exist.

CHAPTER XI

SANDWICH

From Ramsgate per South-East Line Station high up at back of town.

On foot, riding, driving, or biking only one Royal Road to Sandwich, after once having passed "The Sportsman," which is a fair specimen of a wayside inn, with, as at Pegwell and Minster, the inevitable "Tea Gardens."

For equestrians the Sandwich Road is one of the best riding roads all the year round in the island, as you go along the briny littoral on marine turf crackling with small shells; this peculiar turf is always soft, not too soft, but just soft enough, rarely ever frozen or slippery. I *have* seen it frozen in a very severe winter when even the salt water was not proof against the power of Commander Frost.

Then after passing the coastguard station, whose gardens are beautifully kept, where the ducks and geese are prolific, and the homely cat does them no injury, you come upon an undulating stretch of turf, for a short distance on the left, up to a dyke gate, and then both right and left is "good going" in almost all weathers, as far as the next little Traveller's Rest-and-Refreshment House. Just before this, in the most open spot, in the midst of fruitful gardens and with small paddock, is a remarkable house, the proprietor of which must be the very impersonation of hospitality as it is the very openest of open houses. The motto must be "Open house all the year round."

Then over the bridge and up to within a mile and a half of Sandwich is another stretch of "good going."

After this, a farm on the left, and then the ancient Port of Sandwich is in sight, with its swing bridge to allow big craft to pass.

Craftsmen who are past-masters have but to make the masonic sign and see what comes of it.

At all events they will have to pay toll and pass under the ancient gate into our dear, but alas, disfranchised old Sandwich.

This our Sandwich was once very much alive, then it became very much dead. Now King Golf has taken up his quarters here, and the Ancient Game has resuscitated the place, for, except in North Britain, experts say there are no finer links in the United Kingdom than are these on Sandwich Flats.

All theatrical persons are aware of the stage-manager's injunction to "jine your flats." Here the operation has succeeded marvellously, for Deal and Sandwich Flats are so joined together that, to the eye of the amateur, it is well-nigh impossible to say where one begins and t'other ends. If *we* know, we keep it to ourselves as an artistic secret.

* * *

Before seeing anything else in Sandwich make straight for the ancient Church of St. Clement's. If you arrive in Sandwich per rail you will have to pass through the town in order to reach the Church, and in this case your first visit of inspection would be to the Town Hall. But, if you drive from Ramsgate, you will be stopped at the bridge gate-house to pay toll, and then, if luncheon is no object, you will turn to the left outside the town, pass the ancient Fisher's Gate —where the groove of the old portcullis is dis-

SANDWICH

tinctly visible,—likewise the holes in the tower for the performance of the practical joke of pouring out molten lead on unwelcome visitors, and the slits through which the archers took pot-shots at the enemy, and straight on until you come to the first turning on the right.

* * *

This, just after the Barbican aforesaid, will take you up to St. Clement's. The ancient Verger lives close at hand. Send for him and he will tell you all about it.

* * *

St. Clement's is a real treat for ecclesiological antiquarians. Piscinæ perfect. It must have been a large Church ('twas in the keeping of the Benedictines, as, it appears, were most of the Churches in this part of Kent) with many altars. Ask to see the register of births, deaths, and marriages, dating between 1563 and 1666. How thoroughly Dutch the town had become is shown by the names and the descriptions.

* * *

For example, they buried in 1603—
"Debora Boixt, a Flemish maide."
"Katherin Oliver, a Flemish wife."
"Marianne de Powter, a poor Fleming."
"Wharten de Wielson, a Fleming gent."

The Fleming "gent" of the period must have been a sort of Dutch masher. And Katherin Oliver, "a Flemish wife," would be an early specimen of "My old Dutch," whose praises have been sung by Mr. Albert Chevalier. Then there is—

"Siebel Mazred, an ancient maide, 16th September 1623, buried at St. Clement's, Sandwich."

* * *

During Cromwell's time neither priest nor minister was employed to perform marriages. "Persons about to marry" were joined together in wedlock by the Mayor. But the ceremony took place in Church, or the record of it would hardly have been in the register of St. Clement's.

* * *

On St. Peter's Church the Dutch stuck a "bulb," such as is often to be seen in Holland.

SANDWICH

St. Mary's is remarkable, as apparently only half, lengthways, of the Church is used for service.

* * *

But the ordinary guide-books will give you

all these details, suffice it that those who love dawdling fondly among ancient ruins and relics, and spending their time in day-dreams of the past, will find that Sandwich will give them, *à penser*, matter for several lounging visits.

Except at Chester and Trèves on a large scale, I do not remember to have seen walks

"Up and down,
　Round the town,"

so perfect as the promenade by the side of the moat, where there is a wealth of fruit and vegetables sufficient to supply two or three towns, or at all events a very large number of strict vegetarians.

* *

Unless you are fond of the smell of tan, approach cautiously the neighbourhood of the tan-yards without the walls.

* *

If a bit weary of the town take a fly from any one of the inns (I think we got ours at the Lord Warden or The Warden's Arms, hard by the Railway Station) and drive down to the Golf Club. Prepare yourself for this by making the acquaintance of one of its members, who will show you over what are about the best links in England, and if he be hospitably inclined he will entertain you at the Rustic Club; a delightful place. When there ask, first of all, to see their library; then request the Librarian to show you "Boys' History of Kent." It is *the* Boys' Own Book for this County. Ask for it.

* *

Do not linger long in the library of this club,

enticing as is the collection of books. On the occasion of our visit there were three odd volumes under a glass case (it was a sort of letter-box), and the particular volume, "Boys's" aforesaid work, which we had travelled miles to see, wasn't there. On inquiry we found the Secretary had removed it. Further inquiry established the fact that the Secretary had a perfect right to do so, *being owner of the work in question, which he had lent to the Club.*

* * *

Delightful air. Health-giving breeze. Appetising. Just enough danger from the golf balls to lend a little excitement to the otherwise quiet walk. Then return to the town by fly; don't walk, as the way, about a mile and a quarter, is dry and hot; and so will you be.

CHAPTER XII

SANDWICH (*continued*)   "MY OLD DUTCH"

The origin of the name is evident when you walk over the golf links, second to none bar those of St. Andrews.

* * *

It is cut off from Thanet by the River Stour, or as it used to be called at this part "The Wantsume." The poor Wantsume got into low water, and the marsh land from which it gradually receded was probably called Wantsume Moor in the days when England was "Merrie England." Suffice it that the Wantsume retired from partnership, leaving all its "bank deposits" to the fortunate Stour.

* * *

But Sandwich, once a port, is now a good two miles or more from the sea.

* * *

Says T'Otherest Guv'nor to T'Other Guv'nor,

An Interior in the Sandwich Session-House and Town Hall

"Sandwich is a place in which one or two could spend days, and its interesting features would fill a volume."

※ ※ ※

No Sandwich man, *i.e.* resident of Sandwich, could live here five minutes without having a moat in his eye. Of course the ancient formula, "So mote it be," terminated all legal Sandwichian documents.

※ ※ ※

No wonder the Walloons,

"That crew of big breeches,"

flying from persecution, found this "Sandwich and port" so much to their taste. For did it not remind them of their own dear Dutchland? And, when the church tower of St. Peter's tumbled in, is it not probable that the grateful Walloons crowned the new tower with the Dutch bulb that is its ornament up to the present day?

※ ※ ※

To the Court House, where sessions and petty sessions are held. Magnates are the magistrates here, seeing that they have the command of Ramsgate. The Lower Room is scenically most effective. The seats, benches, and panels are of the darkest old oak. Ancient halberds, the

Pity a poor Sandwich man. PM

genuine articles, not "properties," are suspended from beams in the ceiling, over the heads of the prisoners in the dock, who are in full view of the jury in their private box on the prisoners' right.

* * *

The "Upper Chamber," where ordinary cases are heard, is ornamented with portraits and interesting panel-paintings pourtraying the arrival of Dutch William and English Mary at Sandwich. Just the place for the Anglo-Dutch king. The coachmen of royal carriages wear periwigs: Anne receives the Mayor and Corporation, all in black robes. His Worship is distinguished from his Corporation by a light flowing periwig, while some of the accompanying clergy wear powdered periwigs, full bands, and display some finery in lace-work at their wrist-bands. They carry large black hats. The Mace-bearer accompanies the Mayor. Certes in those prosperous times "Sandwich," like "Todgers's" in its Pecksniffian days, "could do it when it chose! mind that!"

* * *

On the wall, on the chimney-piece side of the Upper Chamber, are three-quarter length portraits of sardonic Charles II. in dark flowing periwig (looking anything but the "merry monarch"); Queen Henrietta in curls; James II. in full wig of light colour, gold chain and robes, and in this royal line comes a portrait of John Brown, Mayor of Sandwich, wearing a peculiar collar trimmed with lace, and bearing a wand of office. [*Note.*—He is the only mayor who bears a black-thorn as *a rod* of office. Does not this suggest some skirmishes or Donnybrooks between the Orangemen and the Jacobites?] Then, facing the Bench, as if reminding the justices of the bold deeds of their ancestral Sandwich men, are four pictures of naval engagements between French and Dutch. So unbiassed was the painter's mind that, except after minute search into the details of these works of art, it is difficult to make out whether the French or the Dutch are getting the worst of it.

Here in this Upper Chamber it was our privilege to hear three school-board cases tried. Fancy this in the presence of the life-like presentments of the Stuart kings! Why, it was enough to have called up a smile on the grim countenance of saturnine Charles Stuart of "Merry" Memory!

"Why don't you send the child to school?" asks the clerk, while two magistrates listen and four policemen stand at attention. The public is represented by our two selves and an aimless-looking man who has lounged in by accident under the impression that it was a nice, cool, and comfortable place to go to sleep in. The "summoned" are three poorly-clad women — each one worse than the other in some article of clothing —and some small children of uncertain ages, one being a baby in arms who had to be summoned with its mother.

The general explanation for the women is that they can't manage their families at home and "do work out": that they *must* "work out," and therefore cannot be in two places at once; that if they, the mothers and fathers, don't work, the children won't have any food or clothing and then—*where's your school?*

All which seems to T"Other and T"Otherest unanswerable, though it makes no sort of impression on the comfortable-looking magistrates, or on the official clerk, clearly used to these pleas, or on the police-sergeant who is writing down the examination, or on any of the stolid constabulary, or on the casual visitor by the door, who has dropped off to sleep.

The last case is that of a poor lean woman with a scrubby, mischievous-looking little boy. She is deaf, and every question has first to be shouted *at* her by the clerk, and then *into* her ear by her neighbour whose case has just been disposed of.

* * *

Deaf woman, comprehending at last, becomes very voluble. She is understood to say that " the school board officer called at her house and dared her to leave him " " him " being the urchin in question- " at home." Whereat the urchin sniffs and looks up inquisitively at the chief magistrate, as if asking him, " Now, what have *you* got to say to that ? "

* * *

Deaf woman next goes in for magistrates. For the first time, seeing that she uses only one arm to enforce her oratorical points, we observe that she is carrying a wrapped-up bundle of a baby in the other. She has " three babies at home," she says (Heavens !), " she can't be running after them *all* "—evident—" and this " pointing to the snub-nosed aggressive urchin, " he's not a good boy to *me*, so I tell you." At this point she sniffs violently, hugs the baby-bundle, and shakes her head vindictively at the urchin aforesaid, all at one and the same time. Deaf woman pleads that she " only gets 8s. a week."

Urchin still indifferent. Magistrates whisper, confer, whisper, put their heads together, then decide. All the three summoned ones are cautioned and fined 2s. each and costs.

* * *

Deaf woman protests and expresses her opinion that "it's cruel on her, it is." We, T'Otherest and T'Other, agree: poor thing! only 8s. a week to keep so many children! and if she cannot get work?

Magistrates inform her they are only doing their duty, expressing no opinion of their own as to the nature of the duty in question. T'Other and T'Otherest inclined to yell—" À bas le school-board tyranny!"

* * *

Again magistrates consult; then they so far stretch a point in deaf woman's favour that the hardworking mother of eight who earns 8s. a

week (I didn't catch how much the father might earn, but understood that he was out of work) is permitted to take two weeks to pay the fine of 2s. This explanation having been shouted out to her until the clerk sinks exhausted, she goes away grumbling. On the threshold she stops to shake the urchin who has brought this trouble on her and to give him a last warning within hearing of the court authorities, police included. "The next time," she says vindictively, "you come 'ere, you'll be locked up." Urchin, suddenly overcome, bursts into tears. Exit boy, after mother and baby-bundle, wailing.

* * *

The magistrates inquire "if there are any other cases," casting a suspicious glance at us. The chief constable and clerk, each with a furtive glance at us, as if expecting that we should suddenly jump up and protest or do something extraordinary (from which latter point of view the police are also regarding us), reply "that there *are* no other cases on the paper." Whereupon the Court rises ; we rise. Court evidently much relieved ; so are we.

* * *

We descend to the Lower Chamber. A dear, delightful, old place, darkly panelled with oak, the sombre tone enlivened by a splotch of deep red cushion here and there. General suggestion of a quaint old room in a hostelrie of the Falstaff-cum-Bardolph period. Sandwich without is tranquil ; as Sandwich, except on rare occasions, invariably is. The clerk retires ; the officers withdraw ; the magistrates disappear ; the police disband themselves; the pageant is at an end. "Come like shadows, so depart," and only we remain. We are at work 'tis true, but there is stealing over us an exposition of sleep, which in Sandwich no one has been able to resist. Sandwich itself is drowsy. There is a soothing murmur of dozing life, and we shall gradually fall into a Sandwich sleep, to wake up like two Rip van Winkles fifty years after, only to find Sandwich just as it was when we went to sleep at the close of the nineteenth century.

Curious carving showing a Lion of Sandwich with (apparently) gibus or folding opera-hat

CHAPTER XIII

ASH

A PLEASANT day may be spent by the sojourner at Ramsgate in driving or training thence to Sandwich and then walking more or less across country, a matter of three and a half miles, to the ancient village of Ash.

* * *

The first thing to attract your eye will be the sign of the inn at the entrance of the village, coming in from Sandwich. It is called "The First and Last." I believe this is not uncommon. But what a real "Happy Thought" it must have been to its originator! It suggests the very essence of true hospitality: for is not this inn the first to greet you on your arrival, and the last to wish you good speed on your departure?

ASH

Ash was a Royal Town. Her present most Gracious Majesty when Princess Victoria drove through Ash on her way to Walmer in company with her mother, H.R.H. the Duchess of Kent, *en route* for London and the Throne of England.

* * *

How did Ash come by its name? The ash tree is not *en evidence*. Tobacco in the time of Sir Walter Raleigh may possibly have been introduced here by Dutch traders. If so, the tobacco was long ago smoked out and nothing remains but Ash.

* * *

The story goes that a travelling theatrical company having given several most successful and remunerative performances here, proposed to set up a theatre. The Squire wished it should be called the Theatre Royal, Ash. But when this was abbreviated into "T. R. ASH" the idea was immediately abandoned.

* * *

Apropos of theatres, that charming playwright and learned member of the Heralds' College, J. R. Planché, was very fond of this ancient village, and his book concerning its history and antiquities is the standard work on this "Corner of Kent."

* * *

Ash is built on the slopes of a hill, and the

Ash Church

spire of the fine church which crowns the summit is as distinctly visible to all Thanet as is that of Harrow-on-the-Hill to the surrounding neighbourhood. Few churches in Kent will better repay a visit than will this of Ash. It is as well to get Planché's book and read it up beforehand, as it is probable that the Petronilla who will bring the keys of the church and see you safely in and out of it will not be able to afford you any very satisfactory antiquarian information. "The most ancient portions of the present edifice," writes Planché, "are of quite the close of the twelfth and commencement of thirteenth century." The brasses and monuments are most interesting, and the costumes of the figures are a perfect study.

* * *

"Now a strange thing happened." We were in the churchyard, admiring the extensive view of plain and meadow, pasturage and orchard, all so thoroughly English and so peculiarly Kentish, and happening, somehow or another, to stray away in our conversation to all sorts of topics quite foreign to the locality, we fell a-talking about a mutual friend who was popularly known and spoken of as "J. K." We discussed him, we wondered where he was, as he had not been down in our neighbourhood for a very long time. Suddenly, on turning to leave the grounds, we

came face to face with a plain, upright tombstone, on which were inscribed the two letters "J. K." There was no description of any sort; no date, simply "J. K." We hardly liked to write up to *our* "J. K." and inquire, but we took the earliest opportunity of ascertaining that our friend was still "all alive O," and not resting in the old churchyard of Ash.

From Ash, on another occasion, when you do not want to linger in the church, and when you have the day before you, drive, or ride, to Wickham, Wickham-breaux (where the brewery is), Ickham, then through a few delightfully sequestered little villages, and come out by Grove Ferry. Here a light one-horsed trap (if the horse doesn't object) can be placed on the ferry, and in a few moments you will be at Sarre; thence return by the Canterbury Road to Ramsgate, a matter of eight or nine miles.

En route, between Ash and Sarre, or, in another direction, between Ash and Canterbury, pause for a while at Wingham. Wingham Manor was one of the residences of the Archbishops of Canterbury. Its history has been fully told by Mr. Arthur Hussey in his *Chronicles of Wingham*, wherein you will learn all about the inevitable "Roman Villa," and a good deal about Wat Tyler, Jack Cade, the De Winghams, and the full, true, and particular account of the marriage of that gay widow, the Countess of Kent, with the gallant Sir Eustace Aubrichecourt, and how the Rev. John Ireland, Vicar of Robert atte Brome, got himself into trouble by performing their marriage service.

※ ※ ※

If an equestrian, you cannot plan out a much more enjoyable day, granting fine weather, in early or late summer, than to ride from Ramsgate, by way of Ash, Wickham, Wingham, and so forth, across the Ferry to Sarre, and thence back to Ramsgate by the Canterbury Road. A day well spent; a dinner and a night's repose well earned.

A Plain Dealer

CHAPTER XIV

DEAL

DEAL is a quiet, cosy, comfortable place to stop at, having a great advantage over such other quiet and cosy places as Broadstairs, Westgate, and Birchington on t'other side of Ramsgate, in the possession of a pier where the steamboats stop *en route from* Dover, and occasionally *en route for* Dover. A beautiful shingle beach, dotted all over with pleasure boats hauled up high and dry, and looked after by eligible "shingle gentlemen," viz. the Deal Boatmen. Till lately the Deal Boatmen and the Pilots invariably wore tall chimney-pot hats. Recently I am afraid this quaint fashion has been dropped, and these "toppers" only appear on Sundays, or festivals, and on some local *fête* days when the wearers go round with the hat to some purpose.

It is worth the Kent Coast Visitor's while to discover when the Deal Regatta takes place, with its "Torchlight and Trades' Procession"; and for this and all other information with regard to Deal in general, I should refer him to Mr. A.

DEAL (NORTH END)

S. Vince, who is, or was, the "Hon. Sec.," and who has taken an intelligent, antiquarian, and not unbusinesslike interest in the town for some years past. Deal "can do it well when it likes," and united with its allies Walmer and Kingsdown, it goes in for a "Masquerade" and for "Brilliant Illumination" (what, by the way, would an "illumination" be worth if it was *not* "brilliant"?) "of the Pier, Parades, and Houses on the Line of Route," with "Thousands of Chinese lanterns, coloured fires, and fancy lights." "Thousands," mind you! not "here a light and there a light," but "*everywhere* a light." Then the Deal, Walmer, and Kingsdown Ladies form a Committee and give prizes for the "best decorated or most realistic Car, also for Cycles and Masqueraders." So that the prizes, being given by fair Ladies, must be "fairly awarded."

There is a "Procession Committee," a "Judging Committee" (all ladies)—so we may adapt the line in the old song and render it—

"The Judges are seated, a beautiful show!"

and then come, as by right should come whereever there are "Judges," the "Chief Marshals," who "wear a red band," while "their Lieutenants" are to be distinguished by "a white band round the left arm," and, perhaps, very late in the evening, it may so hap, though disorder is uncommonly rare, that some of them may be further distinguished by white bands round their heads. There are, in the procession, "Horsemen,

Cyclists, Gordon Boys' Band, Sandwich Fire Engine, Trade Cars, Drum and Fife Band, Masqueraders, Old Salts with a Boat, Deal Fire Engine and Escape, Friendly Societies, Druids, Foresters and Oddfellows, His Worship the Mayor, the Town - Clerk and Aldermen in Carriages, Tableau Cars and other Carriages," and finally "Torchbearers."

Among the twenty-six trade cars (really the Lord Mayor's Show in London is not "in it" with this Gala Procession at Deal!) are cars representing "Laundry Working, Arch Cutting, and Herring Hanging," and here occur such good old Kent Coast names, smacking of French and Flemish, as "Bros, Skaidon, Drinkabier, Coppin, Nethersole, and Cavell."

The Shrimpers, those sturdy Plain Dealers, are represented by celebrities of Deal, popularly known as "Stick Up Adams, No Hair Jack, Hobbes Gibbons, Old Seal, Little Hiram, Pigs in the Garden, Tiger Adams, and Snowball." The Show is well worth seeing, as are most shows on occasion; and it is "only once a year," an excuse that may be pleaded for every day in every month from January to December. Plenty of fishing; capital boating; shingly bathing; fine walking; Dover within easy distance, pretty line; eight-mile walk over downs to St. Margaret's Bay, where lunch, rest, be thankful, and return by same route, the view being always varied by the ever-changing sea.

Deal is said to be "the healthiest place in England." Personally I do not think it excels Ramsgate in this respect. Its aspect is much the same as that of Ramsgate, only, like Brer Rabbit, it "lays low"; but as there is a shelving beach, and no rocks, you are immediately in deep water. With enterprise and energy, and by not being above learning, from the best Continental examples, how to make a pier into a place where you can pass an entire day happily without returning to your lodgings or hotel, Deal might, if it liked, after three months of good hard work at improvements, reap a rich reward throughout the remainder of the year. The pier should be extended to begin with, and there should be on it a first-class Restauration; also bookstalls.

Deal has its Golf Links, which abut on those of Sandwich. If Deal improved itself towards Walmer, it could well afford to let the ancient and most interesting features of the town, on the east side, rest unaltered.

CHAPTER XV

COASTING AND INLAND IN SEARCH OF BARFRESTON

Wednesday. *Par bâteau à vapeur*
    de Ramsgate   7.30
À Douvres   arr. 8.45
Douvres   dep. (*par le train*) 9.55
Bishopsbourne   arr. 10.41
    Here get trap if necessary and drive about, seeing what is to be seen, and returning from
Elham   1.46
Douvres   arr. 2.19
Lunch at Lord Warden, Dover   2.30
Dover, L. C. and D.   dep. 5.
Deal   5.25
By steamer from
    Deal about   .   6.30
    Ramsgate   arr. 7.30

This trip fell through at Elham and Barham.

We never got to Bishopsbourne through stupid information.

※ ※

As to what you will "eat, drink, and avoid," that choice is left to the reader. I propose, as your guide, philosopher, and friend, to show you pictures of places round about, and, as the itinerant vendor says of his shrimps, nuts, strawberries, or whatever he has to sell, "You can pick 'em where you like." If you want to "see life," you will choose Bank Holiday at Margate or at Ramsgate. If you don't want to "see life," you can avoid both places at that particular date ; *or*, which is perfectly possible, if you take my advice, you can stay at either place during the most crowded holiday time, and know and see almost as little of the 'Arries and the 'Arriets, the trippers and the touralooralists (with concertinas, songs, and choruses), as if you were in the light-ship, eight miles out at sea, or a hermit crab in his own retired shell.

※ ※

If you "affectionate" a run by rail, try the line from Ramsgate to Dover, then straight away from Dover to Folkestone ; then on the curve round to Elham and Barham.

IN SEARCH OF BARFRESTON

We took this delightful tour by accident. Our one object in life after we had heard of the charms of Barfreston was to find Barfreston. That was our puzzle. It is not down on any mere local railway map. A learned friend, in whose knowledge of this county we placed implicit trust, until our own experience and the interposition of a blunt-spoken, really well-informed casual acquaintance upset our idol, had so mixed up Bishopsbourne, Patricksbourne, and Bekesbourne with Barfreston, that, mapping it out for ourselves,—as our learned idol had *at the last moment* excused himself from accompanying us,—we decided on reaching Barfreston *viâ* Folkestone and Elham (which we connected with the Elham Valley line to Dover), and so ultimately found ourselves about thirty miles in a railway semicircle distant from our proposed destination, though across country from our farthest point of stoppage, we were not more than nine or ten miles out of our calculation. Still nine or ten miles is not a trifle when you are steering, or when you are arranging a day's travel with through connection of trains and vehicles.

* * *

At South-Eastern Railway station, Dover, T'Otherest is delighted at the sight of The Old Guard (or is the ancient interpreter a much-travelled man?) whose expansive breast is covered with medals. We ask him as to time of our train. That is not in his department, he belongs to another and a continental world. He refers us, with courtesy bred of foreign intercourse, to a porter, and the porter is uncertain. After a while the porter pulls himself together, and tells us of a train which goes to Elham and Barham at a certain time. But we know better; that train is not ours, nor is it the one marked in large letters on your board outside the station. "Ah! it's marked up outside the station, is it?" Then clearly this is information that no one *inside* the station is bound to know. We beg him to accompany us to the advertisement in question. He yields, and we are walking with him to the door, when he meets another and a wiser official who takes a larger view of his duties, and who, having seen the announcement, corroborates our statement, and directs us to the platform from which we have to start. It is an excursion train, I fancy, and an extra one. But, except for

"*The Old Guard*"

IN SEARCH OF BARFRESTON

ourselves, and two other listless persons, there are none availing themselves of this excursion. Why? Because, as it turns out, this is the Canterbury Week, and the people have crowded out by previous trains to see the cricket.

* * *

So we have the train pretty well to ourselves.

But we recommend the outing as an outing from Ramsgate. The line is pretty and interesting all the way along. Leaving Dover by London and South-Eastern, you journey along the beachy shore. There are bathers on the shingle. Three of 'em. "Three shingle gentlemen." Retired spots for dabblers in swimming. No bathing machines visible. Novel sight that of an individual in costume of ancient Briton (subject to police regulations) daintily stepping into the sea with a walking stick! I fancy he must also have been wearing an eye-glass, he was looking about so cautiously. What for? crabs, lobsters, or sharks?

* * *

Now we pass the commencement of coal-mining works on the littoral. It may be "littorally" a gigantic success. They say there may be coal for miles inland, and coal under bed of

"An Unencumbered Estate"

sea, right away to Germany. In which case Belgium will meet us half-way. Old King Coal's kingdom will be disturbed: and then the division of the spoils!

* * *

Along the coast, under several tunnels. Now Folkestone. Over roofs of houses — bird's-eye view as we fly along — downs to the right of us — town and sea to the left of us — Folkestone central station. No amount of runs in the cricket field of Canterbury can equal this one first-rate run from Dover to Folkestone.

En route we have been joined by another of our well-informed friends, who knows all about Barfreston. Bear in mind that we are Barfreston-hunting to-day, and that Barfreston is our one aim and object. Our well-informed friend begins by condemning *in toto* the information received from our first well-informed friend, "which," says this one latest adviser emphatically, "is all wrong." He has heard of Barfreston, but having lived a good thirty years in this part of the country, he has never been there. He is sure we shall easily get a trap at Elham (pronounced Eelham), and from there to Barfreston is — well, he couldn't *exactly* (he is so particular as to the precise truth!) say how far, but it is not very far off. We are comforted; our cast has not been utterly wrong.

IN SEARCH OF BARFRESTON 119

Pass Martello Towers. Well-informed friend up in the subject tells us that these Martello towers were built all over the coast by an Italian called Baron Martello. "They don't catch on," he says, "and this particular one is to let." We trust him. But . . .

Mem. The man who knows all about everything is invariably wrong. As the old song says, only adapting the gender, "Trust *him* not, he's fooling thee."

Elham.—We descend. Hail the stationmaster. Will he tell us the shortest way to Barfreston? Stationmaster smiles in his gold lace sleeve. "We ought to have gone on to Barham." Well-informed friend of course says, "Ah, I said so." He had never said a word about it. "Fortunately," quoth the stationmaster, "you have not lost any time, as this being Canterbury Week there is an extra train now coming up and going on to Barham." Bravo! Off to the village of Ingoldsby! for who can hear the name of Barham without calling to mind the Rev. Thomas of the Ilk, whose "Legends" in verse and prose will ever be the delight of jingle-lovers who appreciate wit and humour?

"Of course," says the stationmaster,

reflecting, "you can get to Barfreston from here." "I thought so," cries our learned friend, the Mr. Know-all of our party, "I thought so! We have only to get a trap here" "By all means!" we chorus. The stationmaster considers. "Ah," he says, "there *are* two traps here; at least ordinarily there are, the Grocer's and the Butcher's, and if either–" "Oh," cuts in a sharp boy from the village, "they're both on 'em out an' gone to see the cricket at Canterbury."

"I thought that 'ud be most likely," says the stationmaster. "And I'm afraid wherever you go to-day you'll find everyone away, and gone to Canterbury to see the cricket. Here's the train."

* * *

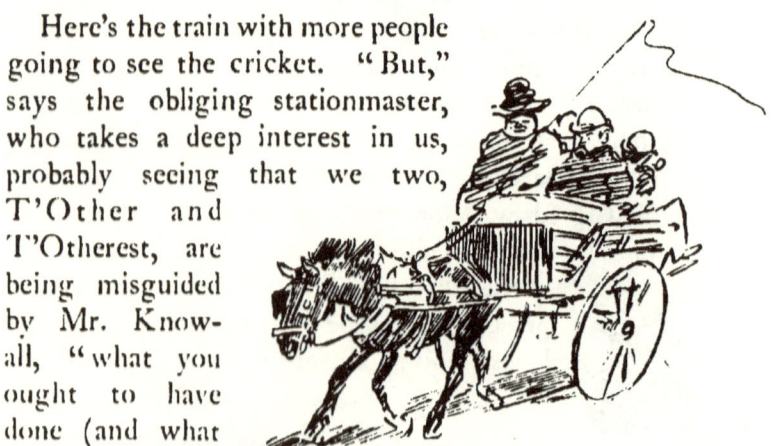

Here's the train with more people going to see the cricket. "But," says the obliging stationmaster, who takes a deep interest in us, probably seeing that we two, T'Other and T'Otherest, are being misguided by Mr. Know-all, "what you ought to have done (and what

IN SEARCH OF BARFRESTON

you *may* be able to do now perhaps) is to have taken a trap from Dover to Barfreston, it's only eight miles." Thanks. Whish! off goes train. Our well-informed Mr. Know-all corroborates the stationmaster. "Yes," says he magisterially, "that's what you ought to have done. In fact, I thought so. But I daresay we shall get a trap at Barham."

* * *

Barham.—All this part of the country is very pretty; the scene truly rural, well worth the visit, if even only to roam about, visit churches, see old inns, and enjoy the absolute tranquillity of this part of the country. Here at Barham we inquire as to trap for Barfreston. Stationmaster, equally as courteous as the one at Elham, suggests that the blacksmith possesses one which he lets out. *Happy thought*— Chorus, "The Village Blacksmith." Without much difficulty, after traversing a lane and a dried-up watercourse, we find the blacksmith's cot-

Smith of Barham.

tage and forge. Apparently no one at home. Fortunately no dogs. We turn into the yard where there is a *débris* of wheels and carts. In distance is somebody in shirt-sleeves talking to somebody else, kind of sporting-looking small farmer. They take no notice of us. We look about for the "trap to let on hire." We attract the attention of blacksmith's assistant. Blacksmith himself out. "But, hasn't he a trap for hire?" "Hm!" meditates assistant with brawny arms, looking about, "hm!" After some consideration, he says, "This is the only one; but," he adds doubtfully, "it would take some time afore it were put together." Certainly it would, if *this* is it. It is an old trap, the wheels are off, and it is lying helplessly on the ground, as though its only destiny were for firewood. "Take some time to put together!" It would take months at least, and then it must be newly painted. Thanks, no; we won't wait while it is being repaired; but we ourselves will repair— to village inn, and there hold

SHEPHERD SWELL

IN SEARCH OF BARFRESTON 123

solemn council. Here we ask how far to Barfreston? Two labouring men and the landlady make calculations. They decide that our best and shortest way to Barfreston, at any time, is to go from Dover to Shepherd's Well, which is on *quite a different line*. Barfreston deferred.

We determine on taking next train back to Dover, lunching late at the Lord Gordon-Warden Hotel, and, being there—*happy thought*—"do Dover and the Castle." This being decided, we return. As we re-pass blacksmith's on our way to station, blacksmith's assistant steps out apologetically and says, "Any other day we should have had our trap in, but master he took it to-day to go over to Canterbury and see the cricket." *Mem.*—Don't expect any attention on the part of the country during Canterbury Cricket Week.

Happy thought—Telegraph to Lord Gordon-Warden for lunch at 2.15. This is good advice to all tourists. Make up your mind where and when you will lunch, or dine, or sup, or whatever it may be, and *immediately* "send a wire to say so."

GIPSY
SKETCHED NEAR
BARFRESTON

CHAPTER XVI

TO ST. MARGARET'S BAY

A "Guide to the Hitherto Undiscovered Sea-Watering Places of England" would be a useful compilation. It would not be such a very small book, but evidently the sooner it is published the better.

* * *

St. Margaret's Bay, for example, could no longer be included in the above-mentioned guide. It *is* discovered; in fact, when, much to my delight, I congratulated myself on having discovered it, I found it already in the hands of a Company, Limited.

* * *

However, as a matter of fact, I, *moi qui parle*, had discovered it years and years ago, only unfortunately I had quite forgotten all about it.

* * *

From Ramsgate by South-East Line, which

unites with London, Chatham, and Dover at Deal—the two "systems" deal with one another here in the friendliest spirit to Martin Mill. Who was Martin, and with whom he had a "Mill," this deponent sayeth not, and no deponent, that I have come across, ever knew anything about it.

* * *

"The Mill" has not exactly "gone to decay, Ben Bolt," to quote the line from "Sweet Alice," but probably it does not do the business it did in former times.

* * *

Remember that St. Margaret's Bay is a good two miles, if not two miles and a half, from Martin Mill station. Therefore write beforehand to either of the two hotels, the upper or the lower one. The name of the upper one is the Granville Arms, and that of the lower is St. Margaret's Bay Hotel Lanzarote. Why "Lanzarote" I do not know; but that is a detail of no importance.

* * *

Pretty country drive to St. Margaret-at-Clyffe. For some distance a sweet scent perfumes the air. Stop and

The oldest inhabitant of St. Margaret.

sniff. It comes from the wild something-or-other which is here found in profusion on the banks by the roadside. The keys of St. Margaret's Church can be obtained at the Post Office, and as the girl who brought them happened to know nothing whatever about the history of the place, we were most grateful for her ignorance, and could give reins to our imagination, as, undisturbed by the sing-song of a professional guide, we strolled through the church, admiring its Norman arches and its characteristics of various periods to our hearts' content. On this occasion a little light-hearted schoolboy accompanied us, who, at first interested, gradually became aweary of our archæological conversation. Outside the western doorway we paused. Here are some sculptured heads in almost perfect preservation. A learned tourist was pointing out to his interested and most serious companions the exquisite art of the sculptor, as shown in the face of a knight or bishop, and to do this, he was attracting the attention of his serious companions by indicating the straightness of the stone nose and the lines of the stone lips with his umbrella. Whereat our little schoolboy, seeing the chance of diversion, rose to the occasion, and from the outskirts of the crowd he piped out in ecstasy, "That's it, chip his nose off! chip his nose off!" All the learned archæologists turned round, horrified. An iconoclastic fiend in their very midst! Fortunately a tombstone, five feet high, hid our imp from their sight, and so he effected his escape uninjured. T'Other and T'Otherest took that boy away and dismissed him with a caution. And a caution is better than a kick.

* * *

Down the precipitous cliff you will drive, or be driven, unless as you proceed it may strike you that walking is preferable. Into the Granville Arms we will not throw ourselves, though the Arms are hospitably open to receive us, and landlord and waiter are ready. The Granville Arms, as the "Upper House," possesses the finer view, and, being midway between summit and lowest point, presents advantages which are denied to the "Lower House."

* * *

But our telegraphic order for lunch had been sent to "Lanzarote," and down to the hostelrie on the beach we were therefore bound to go. Not for the first time was I visiting this hotel, and on both occasions (in spite of some drawbacks remedied in a general way by Moule's Earth—and this defect is common to St. Margaret's Bay, which is, as I am informed, one of the healthiest resorts on the coast), our party enjoyed the fare, found nothing to grumble at in the price, except perhaps in the price of a certain wine,—and came away contented.

* * *

Charming place for retirement. Nothing to do but to bathe from tents or from your bungalow, to sail and row, to fish and take your walks abroad, if, once down on the beach, you can pluck up sufficient courage to climb the rugged rock and gain the downs. Of course there is something else —but not without ascending to the upper air, and that is to go over early to Dover, across to Calais, lunch on the *plage*, *aller en retour* in time for late dinner. With a tourist ticket in summer this trip can be done, lunch included, for just half a sovereign. Save up eighteenpence *per diem* for a week, and spend it in taking your "Sunday out."

* * *

Here on the sea-shore, in light suit and big straw hat, surveying through a telescope the shores of France, just as such a Napoleonic figure might have been seen in the early part of this century standing in a planter's suit on the shore of St. Helena, do we perceive the last scion of the great Kemble family. He welcomes us with an air of resignation. Nay, we have not come

TO ST. MARGARET'S BAY

to disturb thy meditations and thy studies. He brightens up at this, and, to make assurance doubly sure, he courteously volunteers to ascend the pathway with us, to assist in taking our places on the omnibus, without him we should have been left behind, portmanteauless,—and to see us safely off the premises. We accept his offer, and most fortunately obtain the two last seats on the top of the 'bus. It pelts as we drive away from St. Margaret's Bay, and we wave our hands to the Representative of the Great Napoleon, who most heartily speeds the parting guests, and then returns to his hotel on the sea, rejoicing in his solitude.

* *

Truly, as a place for perfect quiet, where the chances against being disturbed by even itinerant musicians must be as eighty-five to one, it would be difficult to find a better than this same Bay of St Margaret's.

"*Come unto these yellow sands*"

CHAPTER XVII

BROADSTAIRS

"You may talk o' London an' Paris and such like towns, but gi'e me Peebles for pleasure," quoth our old friend the homely Scot, and so putting aside Ramsgate and Margate, give us Broadstairs for pleasure of a quiet and reflective sort. In an ordinary summer it is neither too cold nor too warm: in an extra-ordinary summer its sheltered sands become sultry, and only the upper air of the place makes life worth living. It is very nearly equidistant from both Margate and Ramsgate, but a trifle nearer the latter than the former. Charles Dickens loved it; and Bleak House stands out on the promontory, facing south-west; the central point of Broadstairs faces south-east. It is sufficiently satisfactory as a winter resort, though in this respect not equal to southward-facing Ramsgate. No Steamers call here; there is some boating, some fishing. There is neither landing stage for steamers, nor harbour for yachts. A fishing smack having strayed in by accident must remain stranded in the sandy mud, high and damp, until such time as the tide carries it off again. The drives and rides are much the same as those from Ramsgate and Margate. There is, of course, a "Grand Hotel" in a good marine position with pleasant grounds; likewise a Homely Hotel, in the town, old-fashioned and comfortable, with a cheerful sea-frontage, much patronised by such "professional" celebrities as happen to make Broadstairs their headquarters at any time of the year. To Ramsgate from here is a very pleasant walk mostly along the cliff, but of late years the agricultural authorities, *i.e.* farming land owners, have erected a hard-hearted fence on either side of the only pathway, a fence with barbed wire dangerous to man and beast. This "infernal machine" interferes with the liberty of the subject, pedestrian or equestrian, and despoils the lounger of what used to be, but a few years ago, one of the chief attractions of the walk. However, from this purgatorial path the traveller enters upon a free, open, unprotected walk at the edge of the cliff, where there is nothing to prevent him trespassing on the sands below if he chooses to star-gaze and walk over the cliff's edge. This applies to both the Ramsgate and the Broadstairs end. A pleasant walk from Ramsgate, or Margate, along coast; then take train back again, to either starting-point, a matter of five minutes.

"*All roads lead to*"—*Barfreston*

CHAPTER XVIII

TO MARGATE FROM RAMSGATE BY THE ELEVEN O'CLOCK BOAT, AND FROM MARGATE TO BOULOGNE

LOVELY morning in August. Perfect. My friend Grigg and self land on Margate Pier after half an hour's delightful trip, or it may be forty minutes, but on such heavenly mornings time scuds. I give this trip as a model for one of those haphazard jaunts that go so far towards making a holiday memorably pleasant; also just to show what can be done *from* Margate and Ramsgate, if you only go the right way about it, and if, also, the steamboat companies do their share of the business in unexceptionable style.

In order to spend a happy day anywhere *it is best to make your plans as you go along*. The impromptu is the happiest. The unforeseen may surprise, but can never disappoint. Weather may upset the most careful calculations. Indisposition may render futile all elaborately-planned prearrangements.

Carpe diem.

We commence this day by deciding that it is an absolute necessity for us to return to Ramsgate by train at 12.30, so as to be present at lunch. With that idea thoroughly fixed we look about on Margate Pier to see what there is to be done "while we wait." First we bid farewell to the gallant *Laverock* as she departs on her London-bound voyage. Barely midday, and we have a good half-hour before us. Meet Harry Tump and Peter Kinsley. Last persons we expected to see; not by any means the last whom we do see. Tump observes, roysterously, "What a splendid day for Boulogne!" Odd that this should not have occurred to us; but, on consideration, and given the same weather as we are now enjoying, it would be equally true to exclaim, "What a splendid day for Porto Rico, for Edinburgh, for Timbuctoo," and so forth throughout the map. Weather once granted, and sea like the proverbial "mill-pond" (I hate a mill-pond, and the comparison is not at all fair to the sea), why evidently it is a first-rate day for any place—

even London, but it is understood that, in these cases, London is always excepted.

Grigg and self agree with Tump and Kinsley. We don't *say* much : but we respire ; we sniff ; we view the sea, the sky, and the "altogether," and we sensibly, if not visibly, expand.

Then up come two gay sparks, names unknown to me, who slap Grigg on the back heartily, and salute him, "Hallo! my jolly Jack Tar, going across the briny? Lovely day for Boulogne, eh?"

Sketched at Boulogne

Grigg, wincing under the heartiness of the whack on his shoulders, looks at me as he replies to his friends, "Yes, I was just thinking what a first-rate day it would be for a run across."

Oddly enough, exactly the very thought at that very moment in my own mind. I regard my watch; I am dubious. *We must be back by lunch-time.* Clearly if we go to Boulogne we can *not* be back at Ramsgate by lunch-time. At this moment up steams *La Marguerite*. Says Grigg, "I have never been on the *Marguerite*." No more have I. Strange coincidence! Somehow at this moment to go on *La Marguerite* seems to have been up to now the one object of my life.

And—here is the chance! At last! Now or never!

Quoth Tump, sagaciously, "You won't have such a day for the trip again, not if you live for a thousand years!" Thus also Kinsley; the other two haven't a doubt of it. Tump says heartily to us, "Why don't you go?" We return, as if all our happiness depended on Tump's accompanying us, "Are *you* going?" "No," answers Tump decidedly, "I wish I could, but my mother is a bit of an invalid, and as she is only here for the day——" Tump need say no more. Filial affection is ever beautiful, especially in a man of Tump's years and bulk. I notice at this moment that a fair-haired young lady of prepossessing appearance seated just behind Tump (who had risen to speak to us when we first approached) smiles somewhat mischievously as she catches my eye, and then turns away and hides her face behind a sunshade. This of course is not Tump's mother who is "a bit of an invalid and only down for the day," and to whom Tump must devote his entire attention. Oh no, perish the thought! This is not even Tump's sister, nor cousin, nor, indeed, as far as I know, is she even an acquaintance of Tump's, as I do not observe that any sign of recognition passes between them.

And yet—but we haven't time to consider, the

moment has come for decision. It is the closing of Wellington's telescope, it is the "Up Guards and at 'em," it is the moment when the gangway will be withdrawn, and we shall be either on *La Marguerite* bound for Boulogne (splendid title for nautical melodrama in six acts, BOUND FOR BOULOGNE!), or we shall be left on the pier with barely time to catch our return train.

I have no money. Money is no object. Friends have money. It is so lovely and beaming a day that every one is generous, every one will lend. Tump expands. *He* will bestow on me sovereigns to any amount rather than that I should miss this great chance of going to Boulogne—and perhaps be compelled to stay with him—and his mother—on the Margate pier.

Grigg says, "Let's go!"

Immediate decision, "Let's!" Then we scrooge and crowd on to the gangway. We are the last. We explain "no tickets,"—but there is no time for elaborate explanation,—on we go, and—off we go.

We reappear on the quarter-deck or main deck, which it is I don't know, and thence we wave our hands to the one friend whom we leave behind us, namely Tump; and, as the *Marguerite* steams ahead, the last thing I notice on Margate Pier is the figure of Tump bending towards the fair-haired lady as he leads her away

on his arm; and so jaunty is his manner, and in so tripping a style does she step along, that I feel sure of what they are saying to themselves, in duet fashion, "Hurray! got rid of them! wasn't it a lark my (your) telling them that I (you) had to attend to your (my) invalid mother!" And thus are our best feelings trifled with!!

No matter, we are away to Boulogne. It is a splendid vessel. Fine saloons. Bars at convenient distances. A few private cabins. No berths though. Barber's shop and baths. Good accommodation for everybody, and for everything, except for sleeping, as *La Marguerite* is intended for Day Trips only. The feeding better than ordinary; in fact, the way they *can* do things on *La Marguerite* is second only to the *modus vivendi* on board a P. and O., or on one of the biggest liners.

You get three-quarters of an hour at Boulogne if you like to land; some days you may get more, but I fancy these occasions are rare. The passengers form a pretty average mixture of all sorts, but, *if not overcrowded*, there is not a more enjoyable trip, for the ordinarily good sailor, than is this from Margate to Boulogne and back, which occupies you from about one o'clock till 7.30. It is something to know, and something to do; but, *wait, choose your day*, and *then* note if *La Marguerite* is too full to be comfortable. If only three-quarters full, take the trip and be happy. If with friends, you can secure a table to yourselves.

CHAPTER XIX

MARGATE

Midday, August.—Quitting the station (having arrived per London, Calais, and Dover from Ramsgate), T'Other and T'Otherest Guv'nor discuss, as they walk along, the question as to whether the air of Margate—

"It has an air quite its own," remarks T'Otherest, watching the lively crowd with the eye of a sketcher of men and manners.

"Yes," returns T'Other, "an air *per sea*; and to anticipate your replying 'So I per-seave,' I will say it myself and resume my observations. Margate faces due north and therefore when the wind is blowing from the sea there is a——"

MARGATE 141

"Hullo, what's that?" suddenly exclaims T'Otherest, stopping short and sniffing violently.

"It is decidedly *not* ozone," decides T'Other.

"Right," returns T'Otherest, "it's not ozone: it's onions."

"And steak!" adds T'Other with authority.

"The air of Margate *is* appetising" we both agree, and simultaneously we decide on lunching, as soon as possible, after we have "done" the pier and whatever there may be to "do" before feeding-time.

Alas! the north wind faces us, and, as we enter on the road passing by Sanger's Circus and the South-Eastern Station, it most unkindly blows into our nostrils a dry, dusty, second-

The Bellman at Margate.

class livery-stable-like odour which, like love, is "curable by no herbs," as long as there are carts, *char-a-bancs*, flys of all sorts and all ages, and vehicles of every description, including a Margate and Canterbury four-horse coach, all on this crowded scene at the same time, all contributing to keep the odour "going strong."

MARGATE

But on the pier we breathe again, and breathe the very best of invigorating air, as you will also do when you ascend the East Cliff, which is, as from its elevated position it ought to be, highly respectable.

* * *

On a very hot day in summer with a gentle north wind blowing, Margate is a thorough energy-restorer. Mind! you need never be in the rowdi-dowdiness of it—there is not much "dowdiness" but plenty of "Rowdiness"—if you make the East Cliff the starting and returning point of your walks, drives, and rides abroad.

* * *

"Ah!" says a jolly-looking but obstructive matron, pausing in the middle of the pavement and eyeing everything about her as she heaves a sigh expressive of the most intense satisfaction. "Mother!" shrieks a scrubby little boy with a rod and line, and a poor little fish at the end of it, rushing up to his mother triumphantly, "Mother! I've caught a tiddleybrat!" The Maternal heart goes out to the boy. She beams. "Ah!" again she says, drawing another long breath and vaguely eyeing the defunct fish, "Ah! it's good to be alive to-day!"

I'VE CAUGHT A TIDDLEYBRAT.

Poor little fish! Hook'd to make a Margate holiday!

* * *

"Please remember the Grotto." No one should leave Margate without having paid a visit, and sixpence (I think this is the very moderate fee), to "The Grotto." First find your Grotto. Ask a waiter, or a landlord. The Grotto is away from the sea. It is up a hilly street which, being followed, would, I fancy, take you on the road towards Ramsgate. The Grotto is situated about a quarter of an hour's dawdling walk from the pier. It may be more, it is not less. And, "O what a surprise!" How do you expect to enter a grotto? Through rockery? Why, certainly. But the entrance to the Margate Grotto is through crockery, as, to get into it, you have to pass through an old-fashioned low-roofed shop, in which the wares for sale include a large variety of "all sorts," but where the principal business done is in china ornaments and fascinating but harmless toys.

The three Trippers

Shall we say what we expected? Yes. We expected lofty arched roofs—stalactites—deep pellucid waters—fantastic specimens of ancient animal life—and much more of the same sort that Jules Verne would have invented—all for our sixpence! But, "blessed are those who expect nothing," says the Major in Charles O'Malley, " for verily they shall not be disappointed."

* *

We went down as if into a wine-cellar. It was very dark at first, but our ears, on the alert, heard the sound of voices, and on penetrating a few feet farther, we found ourselves in the presence of a fair girl guardian, who was explaining things generally to three young Trippers of some Hebrew Tribe.

* *

The three Trippers interrupted the flow of the maiden's narrative, so that she ceased to take things seriously, and told the crowd of five, ourselves included, that if we were going to laugh at it all, she wouldn't tell us any more. Whereupon we, and the Hebrew Trippers, having all solemnly sworn to be on our best behaviour, began the closest inspection of the walls, apparently built up of brick, oyster-shells, and cement, but principally of oyster-shells. It suggested a long series of oyster-supper parties given by the ancient Romans, the shells having been subsequently concreted by the British workmen, or slaves, executing the orders of eccentric and imperious taskmasters.

* *

"Here," says the Fairy of the grotto, before a small recess, "here you see the places where they worshipped."

On Margate Sands

"Where *who* worshipped?" asks a voice, the owner of which is hidden away in the gloom.

"Oh," answers the Fairy of the grotto, looking from one to the other of the visitors in the front row, who all shook their heads disowning the responsibility of the question which has evidently vexed our guide, "Oh, I don't know 'who worshipped.' Somebody did, I s'pose." And she moves on evidently angered.

And so the earnest inquirer in the dark was left as much in the dark as ever.

We wander along. The Oracle is silent. The spell has been broken. So we, returning and leaving the party still exploring, seek the upper air and the front shop of mixed varieties, where we find the old proprietor, in his shirt-sleeves. He has much to say in praise of his own Grotto, much to be thankful for to Madame Corelli, who it appears, has written something laudatory about it in a novel, and much to grumble about as against his Margate landlord, or the town-council, or at all events some local authorities, by whom, as it seemed to me, the very existence of his Grotto is threatened.

Ascend to the Cliftonville Hotel—that is, if you would be far from the madding crowd during lunch time. If you prefer one of the ancient and well-known hostelries near the pier wherein to take your ease, there is a fair choice. Prices average, refreshment good.

Margate Sands. " How do the trippers come down to the shore?" a great opportunity for the burlesquing versifier to give a new version for Margate of " How the water comes down at Lodore." As to the bathing, they have a good Bathing Establishment (scoring a point over Ramsgate on *this*); but, on the sands, there are nothing but machines; no dapper tents as in France. The men have their own quarters; so have their better halves. You never see, here at least, a bathing party *en famille*. Yet cross over to Calais Plage, only a few hours off, and to quote an ancient refrain—" O

MARGATE

what a difference in the morning!" and how vastly superior to ours are the bathing habits and manners of the French!

* * *

"The Wonders of the Sea-shore!" at Margate. Machines—carts taking bathers up to machines out in deepest water—boats—rowing—sailing—far out fishing—shrimps—sweets—drinks—bands—musicians with tunes—more without—boys on ponies—boys on donkeys—tin pails—bladders—spades—men with "Nougat" largely advertised and doing well—men carrying milk in tins not doing quite so well—water-carriers—goat chaises—miniature Tom Thumb hansom cab with goat harnessed—lovers canoodling in sand-heaps—demure couples

"Won't tike yer 'arf a minute, lidy"

in penny chairs—great preponderance of fairhaired, ruddy-cheeked, sunburnt-to-brick-coloured arms, necks, and hands,—golden-haired girls—straw-colour-haired-maidens and skittish matrons—white yachting caps—red buccaneeresses' caps—caps with names on the band meaning nothing in particular and generally quite inappropriate to wearer—plenty of colour everywhere—

> All that's bright
> Is the artist's delight

from shoes to sunshades—quiet nooks—reading books—then a preacher here—a lecturer there (not well attended either of them, which is a blessing)—soundings of warlike penny-trumpets—newspaper boys in pursuit of their calling and bawling—perambulators—wrangling children—timid children—quiet children—noisy children—dressed children—dirty cupidons without wings—partly-dressed children—laughing children—crying children—altogether happy children—toddlers—babies of all sorts and sizes—shrimpers with nets—lobster-catchers at sea—flags flying—eating and drinking advertised in every possible direction; and, as a moral reminder to the festive public in general to the effect that they had better be careful to-day and think of to-morrow, come the large attractive advertisements, now universal, sometimes on balloons above, or in meadows below, on ships at sea (illuminated for the purpose), on carts, carriages, and walls, all bearing the "strange device" yclept "B**ch*m's P*lls"!!

* * *

The Bathing just below the Cliftonville

MARGATE

Hotel on the East Cliff is good, and rarely overcrowded.

         * *

In fact the bathing all along is satisfactory, and those who take their delight in deep waters can visit the swimming bath, or can go out to sea, and there dive, duck, and swim.

The deep deep C.

BIRCHINGTON FROM WESTGATE

CHAPTER XX

WESTGATE

AFTER the *Tohu-bohu*—an expressive combination making with the hyphen "a noun of multitude"—of Margate Pier, sands, Hall by the Sea, Refreshment Houses of all sorts and conditions, the tourist, tired of "alarums and excursions" (wonderful prophetic vision had the Divine William, even in his stage directions!), will do well to walk or drive to Westgate, of which the first house is about one mile distant from the last house on the extreme border line of Margate. The driver of a local fly will demand a fare that will strike you as excessive, two-and-sixpence for this job. In the words of the glee, adapted in gender to the occasion,

"Trust him not, he's fooling thee,"

and to prevent discussion, it is even best to

ascertain from local authority (the newspaper or a guide-book) what are the regular legal fares for conveyance.

Westgate-on-sea, which ought to be a dressy place, and rather a horsey place too, seeing that the sound of the name suggests *Wesket à coaty de mer*, was built by somebody gifted with a certain amount of architectural taste, and who had at his free disposition any quantity of red bricks, which were becoming a burden for him too heavy to bear. It might be re-entitled "Red-wesket-on-sea."

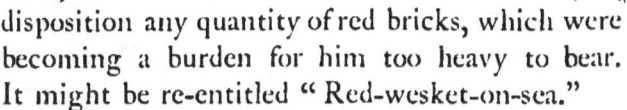

Here is very good bathing in a limited space; not a few hotels all more or less prim and severely respectable; a considerable number of private residences, all occupied during the summer, and well-nigh all deserted in the winter. For Westgate, between November and May, specially if the winter be severe, is like a Beauty the tip of whose exquisite nose has been tweaked by rude Jack Frost; its redness of colour is accentuated painfully, not pleasantly.

Within a degree or so, its aspect is as northerly as that of Margate; but its aspect on a dull winter's day is decidedly not cheery. Its small bathing bay is however fairly protected from the winds, and the sands stretch right away to Birchington and beyond. In this waste of sand I noticed one solitary bathing tent. A few shops suffice apparently for the wants of Westgate. The characteristic feature of Westgate is its gardens and lawns overlooking the sea—or, rather, facing it, as the sea, being a great element in the life of Westgate, cannot exactly be "overlooked."

The Westgate Authorities ("Authorities" is a good word, and like the word "Poltics" in Count Smorltork's book, "surprises by himself" council and vestries *ad lib.*) have done well in providing country seats for visitors. "Country seats" sounds palatial; but the allusion here is to benches in the open air.

Some few residents hibernate here, and still fewer visitors. The hotels, as far as my research reaches, are shut up, as if winter were too good a repartee for them, and they had nothing to say for themselves when once November came on the scene.

There are excellent lawn tennis grounds, and one of the private houses (formerly tenanted by Mr. Orchardson, R.A.) used to have its own covered tennis court; but this of course could not be calculated in a list of public amusements.

Besides lawn tennis and bathing there is limited boating, and for any one whose complaint it suits

WESTGATE 157

to do nothing at all, and do it comfortably, a consulting physician might suggest a worse prescription than a dose of Westgate.

There is no pier: there are no steamers. For these you must go to Margate.

For pony-trappers and for equestrians the place is well provided with excellent livery stables where horses and carriages can be had on fair terms.

The attraction in winter for equestrians, with or without their own horses, is first its proximity to most of the meets of the Thanet Harriers, and, secondly, the first-rate galloping for miles over fields as yet unsown, always taking the precaution to "'ware roots," and then to take other routes where you and your horse will do no harm to even

"*Far from the madding crowd*"
Sketched between Margate and Westgate

a trembling whitefaced turnip. In summer the roads are hard, but the air is always exhilarating, and if you are a bicyclist, as of course you are, there are splendid turnpike roads open to you everywhere. Capital place for learning to "bike."

Birchington, Westgate, and Broadstairs, share between them one great advantage which will be always highly appreciated by the student, or by any one who would fly far away from the madding crowds, and that is, they can only be reached by one line of railway, *i.e.* the London, Chatham, and Dover; consequently on their yellow sands there is nothing like the run that there is on those of Ramsgate and Margate. Westgate-on-sea cannot be archæologically interesting for at least another five centuries, when perhaps the remains of red villas and bicycle tyres will be priceless treasures.

* *

Westgatian amusements. These are, as I have already hinted, mild—as mild as the air is strong. In the afternoon a small band in scarlet uniform discourses sweet music,-- on hearing which strains the visitor, like Shakespeare's heroine, is "never merry,"—selecting the extreme end of the West Cliff for its performance; and, apparently in order not to disturb the musicians, the visitors, at first sight of the red-coated band, considerately seek the East Cliff for their promenade.

Perhaps when T'Other and T'Otherest saw these musicians they were only practising; and indeed I fancy this must have been the case, since practice makes perfect, and their performance was certainly within measurable distance of perfection. As we hearkened, and fled precipitately, the trombone, in whose "depths there is always a deeper still," was having a fine time of it. By favour of the North Wind we heard the trombone-player's part in the performance right along the coast. He "accompanied us" in our walk. He, or at least the deep bass *bom-bom* of his instrument, leaving the treble far behind, and becoming fainter and fainter at every step, followed us almost to Birchington, and here the deep deep C breathed its last, and, like the poor stage-player after his exit, was "heard no more."

* * *

Then we rested. T'Otherest Guv'nor on a rustic bench sketching, T'Other in an agony searching for a pocket-book, *full of notes*, which it now occurred to him for the first time he must have lost by the way. Horror!

* * *

Calm consideration reassured him. The notebook, with all the notes, was left on his study table. So, his present occupation being gone, he sits, and while T'Otherest sketches, T'Other watches the objects of interest.

Stalking a strange bird

The mind of T"Other takes a naturalistic turn, just for exercise. He is meditating on sea birds, when, at the very edge of the precipitous cliff, not more than two yards from where the two explorers are seated, T'Other observes a feather moving. He sees before him a divided feather. He calls T"Otherest's attention to it and requests him, in silent pantomime, to mark it down. It is evidently a rare bird and a big one. Not a word. Not a breath. Hush! *Happy Thought:* Stalk it! Silently and fearsomely, wriggling along, Indian-on-the-track-like, serpent-wise, creeping towards the edge of the cliff. The bird's feathers move a little to the right— to the left— then disappear. Is it a bird that builds in the cliff? Does it live in a hole? Can the intrepid hunters secure it as a living specimen? How? They dare not speak,

WESTGATE 161

nay, scarcely dare they breathe! ... If it cannot be secured, at least they shall both see it, and T'Otherest can take it, with his pencil, as it flies away. Again the feathers pop up: Is it the tail? If not, what part of its plumage can it be? Is it its crest? If so, it must be a kind of Sea-Cockatoo!! It is down again—up again —it waggles—it disappears—. . . . The bold tuft-hunters have crawled to the edge. . . . This is what they saw:

Birds of A feather

The feathers were in the hat of one of the female Love-birds.

Silently the gallant stalkers withdrew; " Not a sound was heard" as they wriggled back again to their bench.

* * *

"'Tis an eager and embracing air!" they whispered to one another, as they respectfully withdrew from the cliff that overhangs "The Lover's Cave."

* * *

They trudge on silently. Then pause, and look back—

"Well-chosen spot," observes one.

"Ripping!" says t'other.

Whereupon they resume their trudge, *multa revolvens*, which ought to be a motto for a Biker.

* * *

'Tis hot and dusty: so will it ever be in August. 'Tis picturesque: so will it ever be at all times of the year.

Parched Travellers.—First P. T.—"I would give five shillings for a whisky and soda."

Second P. T. wishes he had the materials handy, he would let him have 'em at the price.

Then we invent the "Traveller's Companion," whisky and soda glasses complete. The "S. W." patent. To outward appearance, they are field or opera-glasses, with case and strap

WESTGATE

to sling around shoulders. The "whisky-sling" case. Here are the compartments:—

A. small end of glass.
B. patent cork.
C. whisky.
D. soda or other fizzle-wasser.

E. F. G. telescopic extension of glasses *ad infinitum*.

When emptied, to be closed up and returned to case.

If made of aluminium, very light, quite portable and potable.

Traveller with E. S. W. G. at starting *Traveller returning*

Not possessing this admirable invention ready-made to hand, as Minerva sprang out of Jove's brain armed at all points, we wander on, parched and weary, doing our duty of picture-and-note-making, and ready, like true knights of pen and pencil, to perish in the attempt, when suddenly "a sail in sight appears"—that is, a man struggling with a "bike." He is perpendicular, he is slantingdicular, he is overbalanced, he regains his balance, he is head downwards and heels upwards, he is heels downwards and head upwards, and now he is erect, and pausing for breath, on the road. As he wipes the perspiration from his fevered brow, we "hail him with three cheers"! For just at the very moment when we were wishing we could be at a bar (where W. and S. is served), here before us is the gallant defender of injured innocence, or the stern prosecutor of undefeated guilt, in the person of our friend Mr. Jack, as I take leave to style him, leading barrister, terrible to criminals. He is at his own gate, the entrance to a charming bungalow whose cool verandah, which goes right round the house, offers shelter to weary travellers. On the premises are W. and S. and cigars. We stay and chat: then, restored, we resume our way, musingly, making for the other end of Birchington, a few hundred yards, and are received by a charming actress in her marine cottage, whither she retires from time to time and rests on her laurels. There would be good reason for calling her bungalow "The Laurels," but this is not its name.

Birchington, slowly growing, is such a quiet pretty place, cool in summer, seeing that its aspect is north-west, and not perhaps quite so cold in winter as Margate or Westgate

Yet is not even this comparatively secluded spot entirely free from trippers.

The rides and drives from Birchington are of a similar character to the rides and drives from the other side of the island, only that here we have the advantage of beginning with Quex Park, or "Quekes Park," and you are close to some excellent open riding country, Seamark and Birchington being two of the best meets of the Thanet Harriers. In fact, for the special purpose of enjoying runs with this pack you cannot do better than choose Birchington as your residence for the winter. At the close of any Harrier-day you are far more likely to find yourself near Birchington than near Ramsgate, Broadstairs, or Margate. At least such has been my own experience. A mile or so inland, between this and Westgate, is Professor Norman Lockyer's Observatory. I believe his opinion to be that, except on the summit of some remarkably high range, it is difficult to find a clearer atmosphere for taking observations than that of Thanet.

When out with the Harriers in this same clear atmosphere of Thanet, I can answer to having overheard some very strong "observations,"—especially when some sporting "gent," on a guinea-a-day hack, would ride wildly over every field, in bold defiance of shouts from Master, and from Whips, with chorus of talented assistants, "'Ware wheat! 'Ware roots! 'Ware seeds, gentle-*men!*"

* *

An afternoon drive for a fine day in August.— Starting from Ramsgate—to Cliff's End, St. Augustine's Cross, Minster Church; then by Acol to Westgate, Margate, Kingsgate—refreshment at "The Captain Digby," where fine North Foreland view; then by North Foreland Lighthouse, past Stone House, through Broadstairs, St. Peter's, Dumpton Park; then to St. Lawrence, and so on to Ramsgate. This will occupy you, with waits and walks, just about three hours and a half.

CHAPTER XXI

BARFRESTON

WHATEVER you do, or wherever you go, do not leave this corner of Kent without visiting Barfreston. It is not every one who knows Barfreston and Patricksbourne --- the bourne which St. Patrick visited, though there is not a trace of the Irish brogue in the thoroughly Kentish accent of the inhabitants. But that is another story. For the present let your ultimate point be Barfreston. Ask for Barfreston and see that you get there.

Our attempts at reaching Barfreston had proved so often failures, that but for the supreme energy of a final effort we should never have got there. Yet the journey there and back is "*simple comme 'bon jour.*'"

From Ramsgate by early steamer, 7.30, breakfast on board as usual, arriving at Dover by 8.45, and thence by train from Dover town station soon after ten o'clock, arriving at Shepherd's Well by 10.19. At Shepherd's Well you go to the hotel, or rather inn, close by the station, whose landlord, engaged at the moment of our arrival in serving out Kentish ale to two ancient field-labourers, a carter, and a country loafer (with strange tales of what he had heard and seen during his tramping), will accommodate you with a one-horse trap to take you to Barfreston Church, and there await your return.

* * *

A pretty drive, through a country well known in winter time to fox-hounds and harriers, brings us in sight of Barfreston Church, which, being on a hillside, is visible from various points of approach.

No sooner had the ancient church caught our eye than we felt our touring in the Isle of Thanet had not been in vain.

* * *

T"Other and T"Otherest failed several times in consequence of having been misdirected and so gone astray; but when we did find it, we came to stay. At all events we stayed there for nearly three hours, and indeed six would have been well spent within and without those ancient walls, of which T"Otherest made a sketch, while T'Other wandered—in his mind, far away to ancient times when this was a Church of the Benedictines (almost everywhere Benedictines in this part of Kent)— and wandered bodily too about the church, interior and exterior, in rapt admiration.

* * *

For somehow or other this church, or this chapel of a far larger church, did escape, at least to a considerable extent, the rage for reforming and the iconoclastic fury of the ultra-Puritan party which would have abolished all images, statues, and the like, and all musical instruments except their own nasal organs through which they loved to drone the canticles of the conventicle. How they could have abided the word "conventicle" itself, seeing there is a "convent" in it, would be a puzzle, but for the inconsistency of any party, be it what it may, which is indeed its salvation.

* * *

To all to whom the tranquil delight of an ancient church is dear, to all who revel in a day-dream, to all who love to be silent, to ponder, and, undisturbed by verger, by professional explainer, or by any other sort of bore, to sit, to rest, and to be thankful, Barfreston Church on a warm, sunny day in August offers the very haven where they would be.

"I have been there and still would go."

"I'll get the keys of the church," quoth the driver, mentioning the object of his journey as if he were about to call on St. Peter, and forthwith descending from his box and disappearing round a corner, he reappeared so suddenly and unexpectedly as to suggest the idea that a sudden doubt as to our honesty of purpose with regard to the trap and horse had flashed across his mind, and from the way in which he scrambled up on to the box to resume his whip and reins, with the joyful air of one who had never expected to see them again in this world, I am convinced that he was congratulating himself on his alertness.

Perhaps his suspicions were not altogether groundless, as had not I come to "do" the church, and had not T'Otherest Guv'nor, the artist, come "to take it"?

So he drove us up a one-sided shady lane, and halted at the churchyard gate. Then entered to us the Sancta Petronilla, or Lady with the Keys of the church, who, after satisfying herself of our honesty, consented to leave the two Guv'nors free to their own devices, with the

A rough sketch at Pontefract.

church door open, and the entire place and all its contents, including printed description of the church, the vicar's surplice, the hymn-books and prayer-books, Bibles and hassocks, practically at our disposal.

Whereupon we began to enjoy ourselves and to feast our eyes on the church, which is, I should say, the most interesting ecclesiastical relic within a half-circle range of eighteen miles between Ramsgate and Canterbury.

Barfreston Church, as it exists now, is a perfect model of what might have been a private chapel in an old Norman castle. Of course "once upon a time" there was a good deal more of it. However, both exteriorly and interiorly it is in a rare state of preservation. It holds about fifty people comfortably, and would accommodate many more were such chairs as we see in continental churches substituted for the cumbersome desks and benches.

"*As bold as lions, but as ignorant as pigs until they 'card the Gospel*"—Local authority verbatim.

"There are about a hundred people in the parish," the Lady of the Keys informs us, and she gives us to understand that this church has room and to spare for as many of the parishioners as patronise it regularly.

The old stone carvings are almost perfect; so are the delicate traceries and quaintly devised patterns as of fine lace-work. The walls, as shown by the depth of the window-recesses, are a good three feet in thickness. There are a rose window and three small windows in the east end above where the altar once stood, to the left of which is the usual piscina for washing the sacred vessels, and on the right the cupboard for the holy oils.

"*Dragon swallowing his tail, signifying eternity*"—Local authority *verbatim*.

I should surmise that, in old days, the altar did not stand up against the wall as it is now placed. It is of stone, but as there are no altar-marks visible, it is most probably a tomb moved from some other portion of the church. The arched recess, on the south side, with the two strange heads on either side of it, corresponds exactly with the similar arch visible on the exterior ; and so, I should imagine, this was the entrance to another chapel, probably the Lady Chapel, which has entirely disappeared. That the walls were pictorially ornamented in colour,—as in so many of our oldest churches and cathedrals, notably in the abbatial church at St. Albans,—is evident from the results already obtained by the partial cleaning and scraping operations in the east end.

There is a tablet to the memory of Thomas Boys de Barfreston, aged seventy-two, dated 1599, which has been copied and restored. He appears to have been one of the good Boys of the place. There is no *Requiescat in pace* on it, so probably Boys was of the Reformed Form of Religion. Thank goodness, neither white-washing restorers nor fanatic iconoclasts have done much harm here. Outside the Sanctuary in the stone border are quaintly devised carvings suggestive of somewhat mixed designs in the mind of an artist who was well up in the fables of Æsop, in nursery legends of griffins, gryphons (such gryphons! Sir John Tenniel, illustrious illustrator of *Alice in Wonderland*, would delight in them), bogies, and dragons, which he represented as quarrelling among themselves for the possession

Relief sketched in the Church at Barfreston

of fantastic fruit-bearing shrubs, and steeple-chasing after one another over *fleurs-de-lys*, while to judge from one particular design one carver seems to have anticipated a story of "Brer Rabbit" by about eight hundred years or so. Here are to be seen all sorts of eccentric animals, the story of whose origin is probably to be found only in the archives of the Heralds' College, and, perhaps, not always even there.

The two arches right and left of the central one, which are now walled and plastered up, must have been originally open. It only requires the reopening of these, and the removal of all the heavy forms, desks, pulpit, and other modern ecclesiastical "properties," to make the Chapel as nearly perfect as possible. An exact technical description of the carvings will be found in Glynne's *Churches of Kent*, p. 43.

After two hours of church work, interior and exterior, we regain our conveyance, rouse the driver from a midday snooze, who, waking, urges the horse into a rapid trot, and so we reach the station with a good quarter-of-an-hour to spare, even if the train were in time; and with such appetites as nothing but exercise of mind and body in the pure, fresh, hoppy air of Kent, with a touch of the ultramarine briny in it, can give.

On the platform of the up-line T"Other Guv'nor, much to his surprise, recognised the form and features of an Italian Prior, whose head-quarters were, at one time, in Rome.

"What dost thou here, thou worthy Father Prior?" I asked. "Art interested in the restoration of the Church of Our Lady of Barfreston?" But of the proximity of this Norman gem he knew nothing. Again, the Italian ecclesiastic has small admiration for Gothic architecture, and before I could convert him to an appreciation of its beauties, or extract from him a promise that he would make a pilgrimage to this Shrine of Barfreston, the Prior's train (in mediæval times he would have travelled with his own train, but now the London, Chatham, and Dover provides it for him) arrives and he is whirled away. "There is another and a better whirled," murmured T"Otherest Guv'nor as the train departed. Then ours arrived. And oh! how eager were the two Guv'nors to reach Dover and the Lord Gordon Hotel.

In the *Birthplace of Podgers*, J. L. Toole used to have one catch-line through the piece, "I've only an hour for my dinner," and this occurred to T'Other Guv'nor when with Gargantuan appetite, on referring first to train guide, then to porter at hotel, to head-waiter, and to obliging manageress, he found that, owing to circumstances over which the above-mentioned authorities had no control, the two travellers were out of their reckoning by just twenty minutes, and that the gorgeous lunch ordered for Guzzling Jack and Gorging Jimmy by telegram twenty-four hours ago, must be served up and devoured in twenty-five minutes "by Shrewsbury (or any other) clock," and that then we must rush off to catch the only train that could be caught that day, the only train, that is, that would fit in exactly with the arrangement made and provided most thoughtfully beforehand by T'Otherest with the sanction and approval of T'Other.

* * *

Yes, in ancient churches and mediæval buildings, as well as in modern hotels, the "*restauration*" has to be most carefully carried out.

* * *

The rooms at the Lord Gordon Warden are palatial, luxurious, *and* comfortable. Comfort first; luxury after. "Give me," says T'Otherest, disposing of a *côtelette a la soubise*, "the necessary, and I can order the superfluous. Cleanliness first; ready and willing service above and below; a first-rate cuisine and cellar, and I will not ask for marble halls, tapestried walls, jewelled balusters, gold and silver plate to feed on, and bouquets of exotics everywhere. A chop and a pint of stout, if only first-rate, will suffice for me —waiter! a little more of that *perdrix aux choux* —and hey! what?—no *asperges d'Argenteuil!!* —why, confound it, you ought to have this all the year round—they do in Paris!" and therewith he frowns and looks out towards the melancholy ocean, as if there and then he were on the point of ordering up the Calais-Douvres and crossing over in order to fetch the *asperges d'Argenteuil* from Durand's, or chez Voisin. However, better counsels prevail; swallowing his indignation, washed down with a glass of excellent Beaune, he resumes his lunch where he left off, and discourses to us on the difference between continental and English hotels.

* * *

In the main I agree with him. But for the best quality and moderate price combined, the "Pick'd man of Countries," when in Paris or in London, does not go to the most famous and most expensive restaurants, where the *ris de veau* is 15 francs, and the *ris de garçon* is valued at another ten. No: *he* knows where there is quiet, comfort, and a perfect little French dinner, with the very best of wine, with the most fragrant coffee to follow, all excellent, and at a moderate price; and this is a secret which he and a few other *bon vivants à bon marché* keep to themselves and only impart it at the price of a dinner.

There is no hotel which has such chances of showing genuine hospitality as one whose mission it is to receive travellers coming directly from the ship in which they have just crossed the Channel.

To the ladies the Matron should be motherly, nurselike, all sympathy and tenderness; while the Chambermaids should be as sisters of charity, closely following the Lady Superior's example.

For the men the Manager should have everything ready; he should advise, cheer, recommend, and the attendants should do likewise. Baths, hot water, tea, brandies-and-sodas, all should be at hand. The stormier the night, the warmer the display of sympathy; and on such occasions the greater should be the show of eagerness to provide for all wants, and to answer all questions.

In the Hotel Manager's vocabulary there ought to be no such word as "Impossible."

Being at Dover and having lunched well and wisely, "What next?" The answer is, "Hire a fly, drive up to the Castle, and go over it,"—not in the fly of course.

* * *

Well worth drive and visit. See the town itself. There is far more in it than meets the eye of the ordinary Dover-to-Calais and *vice versa* voyagers. It is a pleasant town; life is lively; the drives round about it are through some of the most interesting, the prettiest parts of the Kentish coast land; and for those who love the run over to Calais or to Ostend and back, there is no end to the amusement, except, of course, Ost-end.

* * *

Twenty minutes for refreshment and then "Bang goes Saxpence," and "Off! off! said the stranger,"—and so to swallow several *hors d'œuvres*, devour a capon, with brawn and vegetables, to quaff a flagon of coal-black porter, and to wash down the repast with a deep draught of the best Burgundy was, to our two travellers, the work of a few seconds, and, in less time than it takes me to write this, both Guv'nors had scattered largesse to the crowd, dashed through the hall on to the platform, wrested tickets from clerkly hands, jumped into the train, not when it was in motion, and then, with pipe and tabor—

or rather with pipe and cigar—we, the two Guv'nors aforesaid, lay back on the cushioned seats, breathed again, breathed in fact several times again, so did the Engine, smiled too, that is, we smiled while the engine shrieked and whistled for joy as it sped us on our way back to Ramsgate, where at last we arrived, thankful and happy for our most delightful visit to Barfreston.

**

Avis aux voyageurs.—It is to be done easily from Ramsgate, starting at 7.30 by the boat, or later if by train (or without going to Dover, but going off per Elham Valley at Martin Mill, and so, looping it, round to Shepherd's Well, —*vide notice* " to that effect made and provided "), and back by an earlier train than we, on this occasion, caught, that is, if you can tear yourself away from the sweet restful charm of Mediæval Barfreston Church.

**

Fancy after this to London!!

'Tis to go direct from the twelfth to the nineteenth century!! Still — *il faut* — and London is the bourne to which our travellers must, at some time or another, return.

CHAPTER XXII

THE THANET HARRIERS

The Thanet Harriers offer considerable inducement to lovers of good sport, in a quiet sort of way, with "the currant-jelly dogs," as that eminent sportsman Mr. Jorrocks was wont to term them. For a long time past Mr. Ambrose Collard, of Monkton, has been the Huntsman, and a typical huntsman he is, whether in pink or green. Within the last fifteen years the pack has served a variety of Masters, and so has Ambrose Collard. One Master I remember, who took the pack for a season or two during a sort of interregnum, used to use a whistle instead of a horn, which may be regarded not entirely as a novelty by those who remember Goldsmith's lines about the politician who thus treated his followers—

" He cast off his friends as a huntsman his pack,
  For he knew when he pleas'd he could whistle them
    back."

Still the effect was odd, and the whistle sounded curiously feeble. Personally I have to thank the Thanet Harriers for the exercise by which I

STYLE

considerably benefited, during many a winter season, and Thanet itself for its health-giving invigorating air. "Hare and Air" should be the T. H. motto.

At the present time the Harriers have been taken up, and, so to speak, put on their legs again, by Mr. Percival of Westgate-on-Sea, who has managed to gather round him, according to the report given by *Keble's Gazette* of the meet at the Master's Hunt breakfast, a larger field of subscribers and patrons than has been seen for some time in the island. On this festive occasion Mr. Ambrose Collard told the assembled company that, but for Mr. Percival's coming to the rescue, the Thanet Harriers would have ceased to exist, that is, the Harriers would have gone to the dogs, and the hares would have been out of danger except from gunners. On this occasion this outspoken experienced huntsman gave the neophytes some excellent advice, which, from past personal observation, appears to me to be not by any means unnecessary. He expressed a hope "that those who followed the hounds would remember that everything that looked green could be ridden over, but that they should try and ascertain which were weeds and which were not." Pathetically he implored the gunners not to shoot the hares nor let their friends do so, as it was owing to this that the northern parts of the island were getting uncommonly "short of hares." This "scarcity of hare," he might have added, was a bald fact patent to everybody. He praised Mr. Palmer, a landowner, for preserving hares, and blamed the conduct of some visitors who, after enjoying a

THE "ARRIERS.

day with the Harriers on this gentleman's preserves, went to another part of the island and indulged in shooting what they ought to have hunted. Such conduct Ambrose Collard indignantly denounced as "un-English and unsportsmanlike." Then he begged his hearers to "'ware golf-links," which sounds as though he were proposing to the members of the Hunt the

adornment of their wrist-bands with some peculiar form of fasteners. Next he implored the bicyclists to keep to their own line of country, *i.e.* the highroad, and he strongly recommended bicyclists, people driving, and folks afoot to leave their own dogs at home, as "nothing spoiled sport more than a lot of people with dogs, which ran all over the ground and spoiled the scent, the result being that they (the Master

Huntsman and whips) did not know whether the hounds were hunting a hare, a dog, or a cat."

So that all non-hunters, when they go out to see the Harriers, must leave their dogs and cats behind them; though, by the way, I do not remember ever having seen any one out with a cat.

There are also the West Street Harriers, but their country is outside Thanet, and the meets at a considerable distance from Ramsgate, Margate, Westgate, and the principal places in the island.

The fields in Thanet are open; there are hardly any "nasty hedges and fences," and very little jumping, except here and there a hurdle. In the low marshy country there are awkward ditches with insecure mud-banks which no one ever thinks of negotiating. I once saw an ardent sportsman essay one of these: the taking off was as rotten as the landing, and he emerged with great difficulty, all weeds and mud. Dashing young riders who, like Falstaff, "babble of green fields" (in the midlands), will take occasional hurdles (and be sworn at if they break 'em) just to show the sort of thing to which *they* are accustomed. But these feats of athletic horsemanship impress no regular steady-going member of the Thanet Hunt who comes out for a good gallop, "sees that he gets it," and is perfectly satisfied.

It is this sport especially that adds to the

pleasure and develops the health-giving forces of the Isle of Thanet considered as a winter residence.

* * *

Summary, and Wintry.—When in doubt try the Isle of Thanet. Trust this Guide and be happy.

Printed by R. & R. CLARK, LIMITED, *Edinburgh*

The Advertisements are arranged alphabetically according to locality.

BIRCHINGTON-ON-SEA
Bungalow Hotel

DELIGHTFULLY SITUATED IN SPACIOUS GROUNDS, AND WITH ALL ITS ROOMS ON ONE FLOOR

A Splendid Centre from which Daily Cycling Tours may be made to

CANTERBURY, HERNE BAY, DEAL, SANDWICH, Etc.
and all parts of **THANET**

A MOST COMFORTABLE AND RESTFUL HOME

VERY GOOD CUISINE AND WINES

MODERATE & INCLUSIVE TERMS

Telegraphic Address—" BUNGALOW, BIRCHINGTON "

Deal

Royal Hotel
DEAL

Situated on the Beach

Fine view of the ever-changing Panorama of the Downs

First=class Cuisine   *Moderate Tariff*

Headquarters of the Anchor Sailing Club

Telephone No. 9

ROYAL HOTEL, DEAL

CLARENDON HOTEL

DEAL

Family and Commercial

FACING PIER, AND COMMANDING EXTENSIVE VIEWS OF DOWNS AND FRENCH COAST

Splendid Coffee-Room and well-ventilated Billiard-Room

JOHN ROBINSON, *Proprietor*

BEACH HOUSE, DEAL

FAMILY AND COMMERCIAL HOTEL

Best Position in the Town

Immediately facing the Sea. Close to Pier, and commanding one of the finest Sea Views on the South Coast

Tariff on application to Manager

THE QUEEN'S HOTEL

Telegraphic Address—Adutt, Margate
National Telephone—No. 50

Proprietress—Mrs. LÉON ADUTT

VIEW LOOKING FROM SOUTH-WEST.

HIGH CLIFFE HOTEL

Telegraphic Address—Ozone, Margate
National Telephone—No. 35

Proprietor—EDWARD WILKINSON

The Queen's and High Cliffe Hotels
CLIFTONVILLE
MARGATE

THESE high-class Hotels are now under the same management; and are charmingly situated on the high cliffs in private grounds, surrounded by extensive Tennis Lawns and shrubberies.

Patronised by the leading English and Continental Families

Private Apartments, handsomely furnished en suite, facing the Sea

Famous for Comfort and Superior Cuisine

TABLE D'HOTE AT SEPARATE TABLES FROM 7 P.M.

Handsome Billiard-Room and Lounge lately added

Situated within easy access to the new Golf Links. Special facilities are offered to Golfers residing at these Hotels

Inclusive moderate Terms can be arranged for Families en pension or à la carte on application to the Manager.

A. LÉON ADUTT

FAGG'S
WHITE HART HOTEL
MARGATE

Commanding Magnificent Sea Views

Old Established   *Facing Parade*

Table d'Hote

Quick train ONE HOUR AND FORTY MINUTES from Holborn Viaduct all the year round.

G. MARSHALL,
Proprietor.

THE GROTTO, MARGATE

It is fitting that in a Zigzag Guide a notice should be found of these strange underground Cuttings and Vaults, for the deft Deviser of them planned them in zigzag shape, for reasons hard to fathom. Would that we could recall his Ghost to act as Guide and Interpreter! He might tell us how he came to borrow details and ideas from the old Romans in achieving his lustrous masterpiece of shell-mosaic, and why he has allowed after-generations to wander in this mazy puzzledom without a clue as to his meaning or identity. He might show us how the various archæological suggestions and conflicting modern traditions should be harmonised, solved, or disproved. For 6d. per head enquiring visitors may, on any week day, follow in the wake of the hundreds of thousands who have admired the work, and craved to know more of its creator.

Open from 9 a.m. to 1 p.m., and from 2 to 8 p.m.

AINSLIE BROTHERS

WHOLESALE AND RETAIL BUTCHERS

CONTRACTORS TO HER MAJESTY'S GOVERNMENT

Hotels, Restaurants, Schools, and Private Families supplied at Wholesale Prices. All Meat guaranteed first quality only.

BRANCHES—

62 High Street . .	Margate.
82 Northumberland Road	Cliftonville.
27 High Street .	Ramsgate.
88 King Street .	Do.
13 High Street	Broadstairs.
8 High Street	Canterbury.
53 Biggin Street . .	Dover.
16 Rendezvous Street .	Folkestone.
High Street .	Do.

Herne Bay, Whitstable, Faversham, Ashford, Tunbridge, Hastings, Eastbourne, Brighton, Croydon, Putney, Richmond, Hemel Hempsted, Crouch End, Lewisham, South End, Clacton, Aldershot, Harlesden, London, etc.

COBB & CO.
THE MARGATE BREWERY

Probably no Brewery in England is so well known as the above old-established business of COBB & CO. (founded in 1760), and no doubt this is due to the widespread reputation attained by their Ales, which are brewed from the finest Malt and Hops procurable, and to the fact that for more than a century and a quarter, Margate has been the favourite seaside resort of Londoners of all classes, to whom COBB'S ALE, immortalised in the Ingoldsby Legends, has been "familiar in their mouths as household words," and this popularity is so well maintained, that every year sees a greatly increasing output.

COBB & CO.'s CELEBRATED MARGATE ALES

IN CASK AND BOTTLE

Price List on Application

ALSO WHOLESALE AND RETAIL

WINE AND SPIRIT MERCHANTS

☞ FAMILIES AND VISITORS SUPPLIED

CYCLES! CYCLES!! CYCLES!!!

AT the RACE MEETING held at Rumfield's Track, St. Peter's, on Thursday, 6th May, the two most Important Events of the evening, viz. the Two Miles Open Scratch Race and the Three Miles Handicap, were won by G. Bishop on his "THANET" Safety.

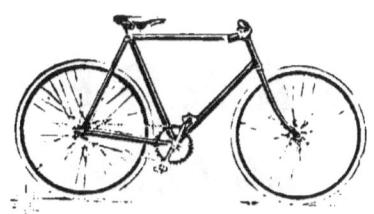

Every Local Racing Event of importance since 1894 won on "THANET" CYCLES.

SOLE MAKERS

OLLIVER & ADDIS

Thanet Cycle Works, Eaton Road

MARGATE

W. J. CLARKE

THE LIBRARY, 37 HIGH STREET MARGATE

CIRCULATING LIBRARY in connection with the
GROSVENOR GALLERY LIBRARY

All the latest works by best authors. Catalogues free on application.

A large assortment of

Views of MARGATE and District

now in stock in various sizes, styles, and prices

PLAIN AND FANCY STATIONERY of every description

Latest Novelties in Leather and Fancy Goods

2d. in the 1s. Discount off all Cloth Books in stock

S. BANGER'S

Original, Celebrated, and Far=famed

ESSENCE & POTTED SHRIMP FACTORY

Opposite the Belle Vue Tavern

PEGWELL BAY

RAMSGATE

Where alone the genuine article can be purchased
Wholesale and Retail

Picturesque Gardens overlooking the Sea

MR. G. A. HILL
Wine & Spirit Merchant
BELLE VUE HOTEL
PEGWELL BAY, RAMSGATE

Noted House for Potted and Essence of Shrimps

RAMSGATE
ST. CLOUD
VICTORIA PARADE, EAST CLIFF

First-Class Private Hotel and Boarding Establishment.   Unique Position.
Magnificent Sea View from every Room
Overlooking Granville Gardens, Band Stand, Piers, Sands, and Harbour
Terms from 35s. weekly or 6s. 6d. daily

Table d'hote 6.30　　　　　　　　　　　*Separate tables*

Address—Miss AUBER.

Crampton's Hotel and Restaurant

FACING THE ROYAL HARBOUR, RAMSGATE

BREAKFASTS, DINNERS, TEAS, AND SUPPERS

À LA CARTE

AT MODERATE FIXED CHARGES

PRIVATE AND SALOON BARS

WINES FROM THE WOOD IN DOCK GLASSES

SPARKLING ALES　　　　　　SPECIAL WHISKIES

CHAMPAGNE ON DRAUGHT

RAMSGATE

PARAGON HOUSE PRIVATE HOTEL

Situated on the West Cliff Promenade facing the Sea

SOUTH AND WEST ASPECTS

60 ROOMS, OF WHICH 40 FACE THE SEA

SANITARY CERTIFICATE

For Terms apply to

Mr. & Mrs. ROSE, Proprietors

RAMSGATE
THE GRANVILLE HOTEL

THE GRANVILLE HOTEL

LARGEST & LEADING HOTEL IN RAMSGATE

The most bracing and invigorating seaside resort in England

Complete system of Baths in the Hotel, including Turkish, Ozone, Douche, Russian, Spray, &c.

CUISINE UNEXCELLED

ONLY TWO HOURS FROM LONDON

The Granville Express leaves Victoria at 3.25 daily, arriving 5.28

CARL G. GRÜNHOLD
Manager

Foy Boat Hotel and Boarding Establishment
Opposite the Tidal Ball
WEST CLIFF, RAMSGATE

FINE SEA VIEW, IMMEDIATELY OVERLOOKING THE ROYAL HARBOUR. ALL ROOMS FACING THE SEA.

Finest Selection of Wines and all Spirits of Best Quality
BASS'S AND ALL BEST LONDON AND BURTON BREWERS' BEERS
Terms Moderate
Proprietors—Mr. and Mrs. HOLLOWAY

The Royal Hotel <small>Good Sea View</small>

For FAMILIES and GENTLEMEN Ramsgate

(FACING THE NEW FRONT ROAD)

A Good Coffee Room, Table d'Hote, and Public Drawing and Smoking Rooms

Within Five Minutes' walk of the L. C. & D. and South-Eastern Railway Stations

THIS FIRST-CLASS HOTEL affords every Domestic Comfort, is situated opposite the Royal Harbour, commanding extensive views of the Goodwin Sands, Downs, etc., and is sheltered from the north-east winds.

This Hotel has been used as a Temporary Residence by the late Duc d'Aumale, the French Imperial Family, and other Royal and distinguished personages.

J. J. ROACH, *Proprietor*

CENTRAL HOTEL

HIGH STREET, RAMSGATE

Bed and Breakfast from 4s. 6d.

Billiards. Two High=Class Tables

London and Burton Ales

Wines and Spirits all best Quality

Proprietor—J. REDHOUSE
(Late of London)

RAMSGATE
VICTORIA HOTEL
HARDRES STREET

FAMILY AND COMMERCIAL

(First-class Temperance)

CENTRAL POSITION   *NIGHT PORTER*

Strictly Moderate Tariff

Telegrams - "Victoria, Ramsgate."   Mrs. J. C. WEEKS
National Telephone—No. 10.   *Manageress*

"Cyclists' Touring Club"

ROYAL PARAGON BATHS
WEST CLIFF, RAMSGATE

Open Daily all the Year round. Warm Sea and Fresh Water Baths.

Hours: **Summer Months, 6.30 a.m. to 8 p.m.; Winter Months, 8 a.m. to 8 p.m. Prices Moderate.**

Largest and Best Ventilated Sea Water Baths in the District.

W. PREWETT, *Proprietor.*

THE QUEEN'S LIBRARY

Cheap Subscriptions   Single Volumes Lent

BLINKO & SON
Booksellers and Stationers
27 QUEEN STREET, RAMSGATE

Photographic Views of RAMSGATE and Neighbourhood

LARGE STOCK OF LEATHER GOODS

TELEPHONE No. 2.

Contracts given for Weddings, Picnic Parties, etc.

J. C. WOODWARD
FLY PROPRIETOR AND JOB MASTER
34 TOWNLEY STREET
WEST CLIFF, RAMSGATE

Carriages for Hire by Day, Hour, or Journey
Station Orders punctually attended to

COWKEEPER AND DAIRYMAN

Orders received at
34 TOWNLEY ST. OR 79 ADDINGTON ST.

Telegrams—"Hodgman, Contractor, Ramsgate."   Telephone—55.

A. D. HODGMAN

JOB MASTER

LIVERY, BAIT, AND COMMISSION STABLES

King's Street Mews, Granville Mews, Albert Mews, Market Place, Willson's Road, Albert Street, Smith's Yard, King Street,

RAMSGATE

Order Offices—78 Queen Street and 30 King Street

Broughams, Victorias, Landaus, Waggonettes, Private Busses, Pair and Four-horse Brakes, Dog Carts and Saddle Horses, by the Hour, Day, Week, or Job. Orders punctually attended to for Carriages to or from the Rail. Horses jobbed for all purposes.

A. D. HODGMAN

REMOVAL CONTRACTOR AND WAREHOUSEMAN

Removing by Road, Rail or Sea, Furniture, Luggage, Pictures, Glass, Musical Instruments, Plate, Wine, Carriages, and every description of Movable Property Warehoused or Removed to and from all parts of the United Kingdom and Continent, in specially-constructed lock-up Vans, from house to house, without packing, trouble, or risk to the Owner.

Special Care taken with Removals by Rail or Sea
All Work personally superintended

78 Queen Street, Ramsgate

LARGEST WAREHOUSE IN THE ISLE OF THANET

Reasonable Terms   **Estimates Free**

SELECT SCHOOL FOR BOYS AT THE SEASIDE

WEST CLIFF SCHOOL, RAMSGATE

Headmaster, A. P. SOUTHEE, A.C.P.

This School affords sound training for professional and commercial life; each pupil receiving individual attention.

Its religious teaching is definitely in accord with the Protestant Principles of the Church of England.

References permitted to several well-known Evangelical Clergymen and to professional and business men in London and Provinces.

The domestic arrangements are under the personal supervision of Mrs. Southee.

Official Tailor for both Ladies and Gentlemen

Geo. Wellden

"THE TAILOR NEXT THE POST OFFICE"

40 HIGH STREET, RAMSGATE

WHO supplies High-Class Materials, combined with the Art of the Tailor, congruous to the needs of Ladies and Gentlemen, at moderate prices.

Shirt Tailoring.   Hygienic Underwear.

Hats by the Best Makers; and all kinds of High-Class and Athletic Outfits.

TRADE MARK

VISITORS TO THE ISLE OF THANET

should secure a length of "SEA SERGE," it is the best and cheapest for the Seaside. The Dye, Price, and Qualities are all that can be desired, and the Serges are for both Ladies and Gentlemen, and excellent for children's wear; the salt water does not harm them, and they are wonderfully strong.

A length of "SEA SERGE" makes an excellent present, and can be obtained only from

GEO. WELLDEN
The Tailor next the Post Office
40 HIGH STREET, RAMSGATE

J. D. Hawkins & Co.

SILK MERCERS

MILLINERY, MANTLE, AND DRESS

WAREHOUSES

11 and 13 QUEEN STREET, RAMSGATE

Costumes and Underclothing

MOURNING ORDERS CAREFULLY EXECUTED

CARPETS, CALICOES, LINENS, SHEETINGS

AND

HOUSEHOLD FURNISHING WAREHOUSE

R. G. DUNN & SONS

High Class Upholsterers

63 & 92 QUEEN STREET

RAMSGATE

For the Largest & Cheapest Stock of

    CARPETS, LINOLEUMS, CURTAINS

    DRAWING-ROOM FURNITURE

    DINING-ROOM FURNITURE

    BEDROOM FURNITURE

    BEDSTEADS, BEDDING

    FANCY GOODS

COMPARISON SOLICITED

THE LARGEST STOCK IN KENT

HEALTHY HOMES

TELEPHONE 41A

MANSION,
VILLA, AND
COTTAGE

SURVEYED AND REPORTED UPON BY

EDMUND R. DUNN, Assoc. San. Inst.

(Registered by the Worshipful Company of Plumbers)

QUALIFIED SANITARY INSPECTOR

(By Certificate of Sanitary Institute)

90 QUEEN STREET, RAMSGATE

DISTANCE NO OBJECT   NOMINAL CHARGES

CONTRACTOR for
HOUSE REPAIRS
and **DECORATIONS**
OF EVERY DESCRIPTION

NOTE THE ADDRESS

2, 4, & 6 QUEEN STREET, RAMSGATE

ESTABLISHED 1804

IMPORTANT SALE

PAGE & SONS

Offer the Whole of their large Stock of

WINES AND SPIRITS

at about the same price as they would realise if sold by

PUBLIC AUCTION

For Net Cash

Delivered free to any part of the Isle of Thanet and to any station on the S.E.R. and L. C. & D. R.

SAMPLES FORWARDED ON APPLICATION

Sole appointed Agents for

MESSRS. MOET & CHANDON'S CHAMPAGNES

ALE AND STOUT BOTTLERS

W. ANDREWS

WHOLESALE AND RETAIL FISHMONGER

ICE AND OYSTER MERCHANT

20 ADDINGTON STREET

Ramsgate

Lobsters and Crabs kept alive in our own Tanks in the Harbour all the year round

LIVE FISH AT EVERY TIDE

Country Orders and Orders by Post receive Prompt Attention

SPECIAL TERMS FOR SCHOOLS AND BOARDING-HOUSES

FAMILIES AND HOTELS WAITED ON DAILY

PRIESTLEY'S
Cycle & Machine Stores
1 & 6 TURNER ST.
RAMSGATE

HIGH-CLASS CYCLES, MAIL CARTS,
PERAMBULATORS, BATH CHAIRS, Etc., FOR
SALE or HIRE
REPAIRS OF EVERY DESCRIPTION
CYCLES MADE TO ORDER. MACHINES BOUGHT OR EXCHANGED.
A large assortment of Accessories kept in Stock
OFFICIAL REPAIRER TO THE C. T. C.

IND, COOPE, & Co.'s

ROMFORD

ALES, COOPER, AND STOUTS

AT LONDON PRICES

OF AGENTS EVERYWHERE

WESTGATE-ON-SEA. — Westcliffe Hotel

Well-appointed Carriages, &c.

This Hotel has an unequalled position facing the Sea, and commands the finest Sea and Land Views to be obtained in Westgate. The Hotel contains spacious Dining, Drawing, and Smoke Rooms. The Private House adjoining has superior Suites for Families (several of which are on the ground-floor).

TENNIS, GOLF   FACING SEA

Every Modern Convenience for the Comfort of Visitors

Table d'Hôte at Separate Tables, 7 p.m.

Visitors received *en pension* **or otherwise**

TARIFF ON APPLICATION TO

GEORGE MARCH, *Proprietor*

Crown 8vo, Cloth, Illustrated, price 2s. 6d.

BRITTANY FOR BRITONS

With the Newest and Practical Information about the towns frequented by the English on the Gulf of St. Malo.

By DOUGLAS SLADEN

Author of "A Japanese Marriage"

"Mr. Douglas Sladen has succeeded in making a guide-book interesting, for his little work is written in a pleasant, chatty way, which gives perhaps a truer idea of the places referred to than a technical treatise."
—*St. James's Budget.*

A. & C. BLACK, SOHO SQUARE, LONDON

AN ANNUAL BIOGRAPHICAL DICTIONARY

Price 3s. 6d. net

WHO'S WHO
1897

FORTY-NINTH YEAR OF ISSUE
(Entirely Remodelled)

EDITED BY

DOUGLAS SLADEN

CONTAINS NEARLY 6000 BIOGRAPHIES—MOSTLY AUTO-BIOGRAPHIES—OF THE LEADING MEN AND WOMEN OF THE DAY, BESIDES BEING

A COMPLETE PEERAGE, BARONETAGE, KNIGHTAGE, &c.

IN CROWN 8vo, 832 PAGES, BOUND IN CLOTH GILT, WITH GILT EDGES AND ROUNDED CORNERS

Price 3s. 6d. net

LONDON: ADAM & CHARLES BLACK, SOHO SQUARE, W.

THE GORDON HOTELS

ARE

GRAND HOTEL .	LONDON
HÔTEL MÉTROPOLE AND WHITEHALL ROOMS	LONDON
HÔTEL VICTORIA	LONDON
FIRST AVENUE HOTEL	LONDON
HÔTEL MÉTROPOLE AND CLARENCE ROOMS	BRIGHTON
BURLINGTON HOTEL .	EASTBOURNE
ROYAL PIER HOTEL .	RYDE, ISLE OF WIGHT
CLIFTONVILLE HOTEL	MARGATE
LORD WARDEN HOTEL	. DOVER
HÔTEL MÉTROPOLE .	FOLKESTONE
HÔTEL MÉTROPOLE .	MONTE CARLO
HÔTEL MÉTROPOLE .	CANNES

NEW NOVELS

A DOZEN WAYS OF LOVE. By Miss L. Dougall.
Author of "Beggars All." Crown 8vo. Cloth. Price 6s.

"In her collection of short stories, 'A Dozen Ways of Love,' Miss Lily Dougall is at her best. The book may be praised almost without reserve. There is no doubt that she possesses the temperament of a genius."—*British Weekly*.

"What is really wonderful about the book is the variety of strangely original situations the author has hit upon. All the tales are good, and each one in turn carries the attention with unflagging interest to the end."—*Guardian*.

OUT OF HER SHROUD. By Henry Ochiltree.
Author of "Redburn." Crown 8vo. Cloth. Price 6s.

The story is one mainly about student and theatrical life during the middle of last century. While partially founded upon fact, it is at the same time largely based on an imaginative outline of the life of the period in Scotland, drawn mostly from a study of the history of that epoch. If at times it may appear to the reader too sensational, it is because the author was himself strongly impressed by the nature of Scottish life then presented and now almost obliterated, but which may still be found in remote parts of the country by those whose affections dwell tenderly on all that is good and of old standing.

A MATTER OF TEMPERAMENT. By Caroline Fothergill. Author of "The Comedy of Cecilia" and "A Question of Degree." Crown 8vo. Cloth. Price 6s.

"A novel with singular originality of idea, and with a daringly unconventional ending."—*Black and White*.

THE JUCKLINS. By Opie Read. Author of "A Kentucky Colonel." Crown 8vo. Cloth. Price 3s. 6d.

"The whole book rings so true, is so manly, so exquisitely written, that I am looking forward with impatience to Mr. Read's next work. I hear that Mr. Read is an American; would that we could have the honour of claiming him as a countryman of our own!"—*To-Day*.

LONDON: A. & C. BLACK, SOHO SQUARE.

Royal National Lifeboat Institution

Incorporated by Royal Charter
Supported solely by Voluntary Contributions

Patron—Her Most Gracious Majesty the Queen

President—HIS GRACE THE DUKE OF NORTHUMBERLAND, K.G.
Chairman—SIR EDWARD BIRKBECK, BART., V.P.
Deputy Chairman—COLONEL FITZ-ROY CLAYTON, V.P.
Secretary—CHARLES DIBDIN, ESQ., F.R.G.S.

APPEAL

THE Committee of the Royal National Lifeboat Institution earnestly appeal to the British Public for Funds to enable them to maintain their **298** Lifeboats now on the Coast and their Crews in the most perfect state of efficiency. This can only be effected by a large and permanent annual income. The Annual Subscriptions, Donations, and Dividends are quite inadequate for the purpose. The Committee are confident that in their endeavour to provide the brave Lifeboatmen, who hazard their own lives in order that they may save others, with the best possible means for carrying on their great work, they will meet with the entire approval of the people of this the greatest maritime country in the world, and that their appeal will not be made in vain, so that the scope and efficiency of our great life-saving service, of which the Nation has always been so proud, may not have to be curtailed.

The Institution granted rewards for the saving of 312 lives by the Lifeboats in 1896, and of 149 lives by fishing and other boats during the same period, the total number of lives, for the saving of which the Institution granted rewards in 1896, being **461**. Total of lives saved, for which Rewards have been granted, from the Establishment of the Institution in 1824 to 31st December 1896, **39,815**.

The cost of a Lifeboat Station is at least **£1050**, which includes **£700** for the Lifeboat and her equipment, including Life-Belts for the crew, and Transporting Carriage for the Lifeboat, and **£350** for the Boat-house (Slipway extra). The approximate annual expense of maintaining a Lifeboat Station is **£100**.

Annual Subscriptions and Donations will be thankfully received by the Secretary, Charles Dibdin, Esq., at the Institution, 14 John Street, Adelphi, London, W.C.; by the Bankers of the Institution, Messrs. Coutts and Co., 59 Strand; by all the other Bankers in the United Kingdom; and by all the Lifeboat Branches.

SOUTH-EASTERN RAILWAY

CHIEF LONDON STATIONS
CHARING CROSS (West End).   **CANNON STREET** (City).
LONDON BRIDGE.

SUMMER ARRANGEMENTS

Cheap Fast Trains (1st and 3rd class only) between **London** and **Canterbury, Ramsgate, Margate, Sandwich** and **Deal,** run every Week-day during the Summer. Return Tickets for the above are available for the return journey on the same or following day, and those issued on the Friday or Saturday are available for return up to and including the following Monday.

Sunday Excursions.—A Cheap Day Excursion (1st and 3rd class) **runs every Sunday** during the Summer from **London** to **Canterbury, Ramsgate, Margate, Sandwich,** and **Deal.**

A **Cheap Day Excursion** runs to the same stations **every Monday** during the Summer (with the exception of Bank Holiday).

For Fares and further particulars see Bills and Summer Programme

ALFRED WILLIS
Manager, Passenger Department

www.ingramcontent.com/pod-product-compliance
Lightning Source LLC
Chambersburg PA
CBHW021838230426
43669CB00008B/1008